Healing Now

by

Mary Katherine MacDougall

UNITY BOOKS
UNITY VILLAGE, MISSOURI

Standard Book Number 87159-136-7
Library of Congress Card Number 70-120120

Contents

I
Healing Is Possible
Health Is a Divine Right

Our life is filled with needs for healing. We need to be healed in so many ways.

There are times when we need physical healings. Sometimes we need only a little healing; at other times we need to have a chronic condition healed; and then there are times when our need is desperate, immediate. Other things in our life frequently cry out for healing too.

Our feelings get hurt. Oh, how we want them healed! A relationship is broken and our life is shaken. Our finances often suffer "accidents." Many nights we spend worrying, fearful, resentful, regretful, remorseful, ready to give anything for a healing of circumstances or events. We were born needing healing.

Babies cry for milk to heal hunger pangs. When children are frightened or hurt, they scream for a parent's protection and presence. Always there is this crying out for healing, a reaching out for someone or something, some change in circumstances, a magical concoction or treatment, a miracle outside ourself that will heal.

Often in our hurt, fever, or pain we think with deep longing for the touch of Christ Jesus or the brush of His garment. We wish that we might have been one of the many who were "touched [and] . . . made whole." Despite medical or nursing attention, we have this very real desire for more. We yearn for a healing Presence. Until we find this Presence within us, we continue to cry out and reach out for healing.

We get comfort and sometimes healing from studying the healings brought about by the Christ. We are encouraged, given hope for the possibility of our own healing, because He taught and preached and healed "every disease and every infirmity." We rejoice with the blind who saw, the lame who walked, the dead who rose. We are glad that it all happened—but it seems very far away, and so long ago. Our healing need is here and now. We hurt, we see what is wrong in our body; the possibility for spiritual healing doesn't seem real. Even when we know the Truth about ourself and about our relationship with God, our Father, we don't connect it with the possibility for healing and health; yet this is the Truth that heals.

We are spiritual beings first, before we are mental, emotional, and physical persons. It is this spiritual self that is perfect and whole, always, for it is the self created in the image and likeness of God. This real self is the pattern for the physical self; it can never be harmed, and because of this the physical body can be repaired and restored. The mold is there. Our prayers and our desires provide the building materials. Since the spiritual is the beginning, the creator, the healing is done through the spiritual. It is as simple as that. It is as difficult to comprehend as that. It is difficult for most of us because we are living in such a material world. Physical ways, physical demands, physical appearances all make spiritual man seem "not there." But he *is* there, our spiritual man. And that is what this book is all about.

The first part contains accounts of healings in every department of life, from habits and memories to finances, failures to faith, our relationship with God as well as physical conditions. The people whose stories are told here found that healing was their divine right, and that healing was possible spiritually no matter what their condition was. They learned the danger of thinking about sickness; they learned to look closely at themselves to discover if they might be *wanting* to be sick, if anything in their thinking was attracting sick conditions to them. They not only cured undesirable conditions; they established permanent health. They learned what it means to say that one's body is the temple of the living God, that one's body is the holy Temple. They learned not only how to heal but how to prevent discordant conditions. Perhaps one of the happiest things they discovered was how to be channels for healing for other people they cared about.

The last part of the book has specific helps for many physical problems. The spiritual cause is suggested, and the denials and affirmations are given that prove effective in bringing about healings. Both kinds of help are needed if we are going to be scientific in our approach to spiritual healing. We need to know and be able to recognize the metaphysical causes of ailments. When we do, it is easier to know the spiritual remedy to apply. Sufficient healing truths and healing statements are included to give help and ideas to use in any case that might come to our attention.

There is a tendency for us to hesitate to learn about spiritual healing, despite our wanting and needing to know about it. There are several reasons for this hesitancy. We know of some spiritual healings today, some faith healings; we may have experienced such a healing ourself; but the healings we know the most about (and believe in) are those effected by Jesus Christ, long ago. More churches today are including spiritual healing in their programs than since the time of the early Christians, and this is wonderful. Through the years, for the most part, orthodox churches have frowned on faith healings. Instead they have promoted the idea that there is merit in suffering, that pain purifies, that enduring affliction makes one more saintly. And all through the years there has been the notion that sickness comes from God, that physical burdens are to be expected, not healing and health. We have all been told in loving sympathy during times of physical need: "You will come through this. God never sends more than you can handle or bear."

What a God that would be . . . a God who spends His time weighing possibilities for endurance, personal tensile strength. No wonder *that* God died! Not long ago a woman called for help in a grave situation. Doctors had told the family they could do nothing more for the mother. Six years before the woman had been operated on successfully for cancer. The family was jubilant. Now with this development, they were about to lose their religion, and they were devout churchgoers. They had been praying every day, and now to have this happen!

One daughter said, "If she dies, I'm through with praying." The next moment she was telling God what she would do if He brought her mother through this crisis. Somehow I could not help thinking that they were treating their God very much as some people do a pet dog: they forget the dog most of the time, then they think of him and whistle! (From what I was told I knew that health laws had not been observed, that the mother had continued to be a chain smoker.) At one time or another, most of us are guilty of breaking God's laws (as well as physical laws) and then whistling for God to come get us out of the mess we've gotten ourselves into.

We overeat, overwork, or undereat; we put harmful substances into our bodies; we breathe foul air, we hurry, we get angry—and then we think that an affirmation will make us healthy and sound again. Yes, we often get so far from God that we are out of hearing. We know better. We shouldn't have to ask whether God sends suffering, when we know that Jesus Christ healed. If healing had not been right, He would not have done so. And we know that God is all good.

It is wonderful that in many languages the name for God is "good." Since He is all good, then He can know nothing but good. Sickness of any kind—disease, hurt, hate, bad habits, broken relationships—is not good, so God can be no part of it.

Certainly some people who have severe health conditions become saintlike and do fantastic things under horrendous physical handicaps. I am thinking of a lovely woman who had a progressive muscular disease that doctors did not name. I saw her get thinner, sweeter, dearer. Even as a young child I knew that this did not have to be. I had an idea that there had to be a word, something felt or thought, that could make her get up from her bed and again be the vibrant person I had first known. I had this same deep feeling three other times before I began to know what was inside me, trying to tell me the Truth about sickness and all kinds of disease.

When my mother was ill, everyone except me was thinking and saying, "Death, death, death." Her illness looked hopeless, I knew even then, but I couldn't think so. I also knew that she did not accept such a view for a long time, much longer than the others thought possible. I knew the moment when she let this death-thought into her consciousness. Within a week she was gone. Even during her last few hours I had this swelling feeling inside: "There is a word, there is something that could stop this death process."

I felt this again when my husband died. I even felt there was a word I could say that would bring life back after he had passed. Naturally, I did not tell anyone else. I doubted that anyone else could understand.

Then the young principal I worked under had several professional blows, family sickness, lost his job, then cancer. I had known him since we were freshmen in college. I liked him. He had made his way through college and had helped support his family too. He was continuing to help his parents as well as going on with graduate work during vacations. Again this feeling come over me. By this time I knew more about Truth. I was beginning to see Truth work. The desire to be a channel of help intensified until I had to make a simple outline of what I believed and why. I went to talk to his wife, who was also my friend. I was rebuffed and shown the door. Roy died a short time later; he should not have.

In not one of these deaths did I see God's hand or design. I could not think that any one of them was

His will. God's will has nothing at all to do with the need for healing that we may have, no matter what that need is. The only part God's will plays is to help us get well. His will for us is always good; it could be nothing else, for He is good. He sees only good for us, He has only good prepared for us. This good must include health of body, mind, emotions, finances, relationships, anything and everything that has to do with us and our personal affairs. If we doubt this, we can help ourself believe it by using the following affirmation:

My Father's will for me is perfect health. I let His will be done in me and I am healed now. Or, *I let His will be done in this situation and it is perfectly healed now.*

For some of us this is a new idea, but it is a logical one, and we know it must be true if God is really the good Father that He is. Our claiming it to be true will help us know that it is so.

The Bible gives us many indications that we are supposed to be healthy and to live a healthful life. If we study the Mosaic laws, we note how many have to do with health. It was essential that the Israelites keep their bodies in good condition. They were traveling in a desert land. They faced daily hardships. The rest of the laws had to do with avoidance of wrongdoing (besides the instructions for worship). Wrongdoing meant wrong emotions and wrong thinking, which would lead to sickness and disease. Constantly the Children of Israel were reminded that they must be without sin. Miriam was not healed until she repented of the wrong done while Moses was on the mountaintop. This has been a common idea among all peoples: sin, wrong thinking, sickness. Even the early Greeks believed that all illness was the result of sin which must be expiated or interceded for.

All through the Old Testament runs a current of healing and the promise of healing: "I am the Lord, your healer." "The Lord heard . . . and healed." "Thou hast healed me."

"Bless the Lord, O my soul,
and forget not all his benefits,
who forgives all your iniquity,
who heals all your diseases."

There is the wonderful promise in Malachi: "the sun of righteousness shall rise, with healing in its wings."

In the New Testament, healings continue. There are repetitions of Jesus' healing: "He had compassion on them, and healed their sick." Peter too had many with various diseases come to him and "they were all healed." Paul "putting his hands on [Publius] healed him." James wrote, "the prayer of faith will save the sick man, and the Lord will raise him up; . . . pray one for another, that you may be healed." In the Revelation, John describes the tree of life: "the leaves of the tree were for the healing of the nations."

The Bible tells us much and promises us a great deal about healing; but we do not have to go to the Bible to know that God wants us to be whole and healthy in body, mind, emotions, and affairs. Our body is so created that the moment anything happens to it—a cut, a burn, a shock—the built-in repair system starts to work. When we are upset, we are so created that we can be calmed, diverted. Even circumstances seem to have a similar natural ability to settle down, no matter how disturbing they may get.

Marge had always felt as if she were a child of God, but she had never thought that she had inherited any God qualities. Certainly she hadn't thought about having "the gift of healing." She realized that Jesus Christ's healing power came through His complete acceptance of His at-one-ment with the Father. She was ready to accept the fact that she too could have this oneness, and that she could be a channel for healing. She was eager to believe that by claiming her spiritual selfhood, physical healing would follow. She had a back condition that gave her trouble much of the time. Knowing the power of her word, and knowing that words are boomerangs going out only to come back bringing with them what we have said, she became very careful. She stopped talking about "*her* back trouble."

She no longer wanted to own it. She tried to put as much feeling into talking about her expectancy of health as she had in complaining about aches and pains before. She used these affirmations:

"I am the perfect offspring of God and I am one with His healing power, which is now taking care of my back and everything that needs healing in my life."

Marge had accepted the possibility of spiritual healing and she was expecting it. She refused to be disturbed by any discomfort that lingered. She continued to expect a complete healing and to know that it was on its way. She added these statements:

"I know that all can be healed now. I am ready for healing to happen to me. I accept my healing now. I am healed, thank God, I am healed! No more suffering, no more pain!"

To help us remember that there is this divine

possibility for healing, we can repeat over and over: *"I am the child of God. I am part of all that He is. I am as He is. He is Spirit; I am Spirit. I am truly His child. I believe it now. I feel it now. I know it now. I am the child of God."*

We will never be the same again—and we will know that any needed healing in any part of our life can be accomplished. Yes, healing is divinely possible for us.

Whatever in our life needs healing, we know now that it can be healed.

My body can be healed now, thank God.

My finances can be healed now, thank God.

My business can be healed now, thank God.

My personal relationships can be healed now, thank God.

My past can be healed now, thank God.

My bad habits can be healed now, thank God.

I can help others to health now, thank God.

My health can be permanently good now, thank God.

Thank God for my divine inheritance of healing!

II
Wanting to Be Sick

It seems ridiculous that anyone would want to be sick, ever, but many of us do. Some of us know it; some of us may suspect the truth; but a lot of us would be very surprised to realize that sicknesses come to us because we want them . . . *because they bring us something we can't get in any other way.*

Sometimes we're sick because that is the way we get attention and care; sometimes it is so we can avoid doing something we don't want to do; sometimes it is simply a means of getting away from too much pressure or work. Of course, sometimes a person is so interested in what is going on in his body that he becomes a hypochondriac; but the ones we are concerned with now are the people who have sick consciousnesses and don't know it; who do not realize that they have invited illness and are holding their own ill health because, whether they are aware of it or not, they want to be sick.

There are many reasons for our having a sick consciousness. For some of us, it is because we are overprotected and sheltered as children. Perhaps everything in our home was germ-and disease-oriented. Perhaps much time was spent talking about diseases and physical dangers. Publicity about health conditions can feed our concern with sickness. A family with a history of certain diseases often sets the stage for a specific disease consciousness. Children grow up expecting the possibility of contracting the family weakness. What we hear and read about diseases can stay dormant in our subconscious a long time.

Anne Roberts' blood pressure was so low that "it hardly records," she told me. "You should see all the things I take and eat, and don't eat." She made a face. "I do exactly as I am told. I *am* better, but it's taking so long . . ."

She thought about the possibility that a hidden desire not to be well was the cause of her delayed healing. "I don't think so," she said slowly, "but I don't mind trying to find out. I truly do not want to keep on feeling this way. Maybe it's only my conscious mind that wants to be well. We'll see."

She was surprised when she discovered that very likely her illness was being accepted because of a certain situation. Two aunts whom she loved dearly had been sickly. Anne liked to go see them and help take care of them. "They were so pretty and so sweet. I felt that angels must be like them. They never raised their voices, they never moved quickly, everything was in order about them. They had a wonderful housekeeper who took excellent care of them and the house. Mother always told me I was more like them than her. My mother was hearty and never sick, always happy. Our household with seven children was always noisy and never in order."

Evidently Anne's deep feeling nature had picked up her love for the aunts and their calm household *where the women were not strong*. Anne didn't quite believe it, but she did want to be well. "With God's help, I will be," she said. She used these statements:

"The strength of the Lord is mine. Nothing, no memory, no hidden desire, nothing can keep me from my God-given health now. I have new vitality, new energy, perfect health now."

Her strength returned, her blood pressure became normal, her vitality was renewed. She was happy, and she was free from more than the debilitating low blood pressure. She was free from any notion that the condition would ever return. It hasn't.

Most of us think it foolish that we would want to suffer, but it happens so often that we all need to watch for the possibility. A man told me how ashamed he was when he discovered that he was pushing back Truth ideas so he could stay sick. All the time he thought he was using Truth; now he knew that what he was doing was *postponing using it so that he wouldn't get well too fast and have to go back to work!* When he realized this, it did not take him any time at all to "get with" his health affirmations, and healing came quickly. We're likely to fool ourselves in health matters.

This may go back to our childhood, where we could get attention when we were sickly that we couldn't get any other time. Even when we are too big to be rocked, we like to be rocked. So the pattern begins—and whenever our subconscious decides we need to have a little pampering, poof! We're sick again. This can happen even if we live alone. We can get enjoyment from being sorry for ourselves for being sick and for being alone. My friend admitted that he liked the attention he got from his family while he was at home; he particularly liked being away from the pressures of his job. It would have been more practical to take a long weekend of pleasure than go to the trouble of being sick.

A woman executive did exactly that. When she felt she was going to be sick, she recognized the symptoms for what they were, whether they were sneezes or headaches. She knew her body was protesting the pressures of her work and wanting some loving attention. She took some of her sick leave, asked friends not to call her, and went to bed. One time she slept for two days. Her only "medicine" was knowing that she was not sick and that her body was being revitalized and re-energized by the healing power of God.

A story about the late great actress, Ethel Barrymore, contained what she termed her "recipe" for her continuing, amazing vitality. Once a month, the grand lady of the theater took two days off from everybody and everything. She disconnected her phone, the doorbell, and herself from her active life. She slept, read, thought. She gave her body a rest by drinking only fruit juices when she wanted them. Evidently she too had discovered that it is better to pamper oneself sensibly than to go through the unpleasantness of being sick.

Jack Henderson had a cold that hung on and on, accompanied by sinus irritation. He had "doctored" and "vitamined" and thought he was using his Truth. He was getting pampering only from his four-year-old daughter, and it was difficult to think he would let himself stay as miserable as he was simply for her loving attention each evening. He was game, however, to find out. He prayed: "*Father, if there is anything in me holding back my healing, I want it dissolved now. Help me to be completely free to be healed now. I do not want to be sick. No, I don't! I want to be well now, all well. Thank You for all Your answered prayers for me and my family.*"

He prayed all the way home. He had only a shadow of a headache left when he got there. He felt better than he had in many weeks. He wanted to run and jump, shout and sing: "I am free, thank God, I am free! I don't hurt. I can breathe."

Sometimes relief takes a little longer . . . often because we don't want to face the fact that we have been delaying our healing ourself because down deep inside we *want* to be sick for some reason.

Two men kept themselves in a sick consciousness because of pensions. One received a veteran's compensation, the other an industrial accident pension. Neither had been Truth students when they were hurt; both became good ones. Health improved in both cases. One became frightened because he was getting well; he didn't want to face earning all his livelihood. The other had a debate within himself, but he couldn't go on. He applied for reexamination, saying that he believed he no longer had the disabilities that were on his record. It took him a little time to get started again, making his own way, but he did. His sick consciousness was gone forever. The other man continued to have many little illnesses, almost as if it were necessary to prove that he was truly not very strong.

We have all known people and families with this kind of sick consciousness. They either do things to avoid sickness, or everybody is always sick. Sickness is, in either case, the center of interest and concern. Suggestions about sickness that we do not realize we have taken into our subconscious can seduce us.

We have to be very careful, for the smallest sick consciousness can cause us misery, and all unnecessarily. Emotion-charged affirmations and denials are needed when we suspect or discover that emotions are holding back our healings. These have been used by many people with happy results:

"I want to be healed right now. I deeply desire healing now. I do not want to ever be sick [or hurt or unhappy or disappointed] again. This is the last time. My whole being wants health and wholeness. There is only one thought and one desire in my mind, body, and emotions: health, healing, wholeness now. I want to be healed now!"

None of us needs insurance statistics or the results of scientific research projects into the causes of accidents to know that on the highway and in the kitchen more people are hurt when emotionally upset than at any other times. Some people seem to be more likely to have accidents than others. They are also likely to have more emotional problems. When we have a accident, minor or major, we are ready to admit with the statistics: "Yes, we were in too big a hurry; yes, we were angry; yes, we were full of resentment or hatred; yes, we were tired, tired, tired." But now research is asking the Truth question: "Did the accident happen because we really wanted an accident to happen?"

Ridiculous? Yes. Impossible? No. Scratches on the side of her car showed how close to a bad accident one young woman had been. This happened not once but three times. "I'm always having close shaves," she said. A man said to me after he had been hit broadside: "I always knew I'd get clobbered that way one day. I could see it happening." Both of these persons had set the stage for accidents and near-accidents. One had even visualized what would happen, the other claimed that she always had these near-misses. If we want things to happen to us, they will. If we really don't want them, then if we have an accident, we quickly deny any feeling of "this always happens to me." We don't want it "always" happening to us . . . not even one more time.

Father, this is not going to happen to me again. I do not want it ever to repeat in my experience. Thank You, Father, for Your protection and healing.

A woman did not like to ride with her husband who was reckless. Neither did she like his frequently saying, whenever they saw an accident, "That's probably the way I'll go," or, "When I go, that's the way I want to go."

Often when a person speaks this way he really doesn't mean it—but his subconscious mind cannot tell a serious statement from a kidding one. It swallows them all, and then brings into reality things said to be desired. There are also people who have a sickness or accident consciousness, and know it to the extent that they expect unpleasant and disappointing things to happen to them.

A young woman had had a long series of accidents, disappointments, minor and major catastrophes. She sincerely felt there was something about her that attracted the worst of everything. She felt she was always the one who got the short end of things. Judging by appearances, she had.

She was sure that she wanted to have things change. She certainly didn't want any more of what she had had. It is good to ask ourself if we really do want a healing of body or affairs. Even Jesus did this. He asked the man at the pool if he wanted to be made whole. Sometimes we have to get specific; "Do I want to get healed this moment? Would it be a disappointment in any way if I had to get up from my bed now because I am no longer sick?"

The young woman prayed this way: "Father, help me stop kidding myself, if I am. Help me to know the truth about all these things that have happened to me. If I am attracting these things to me, help me to clean out my subconscious desires or attitudes or notions and replace them with ideas that will attract only good to me from now on. I don't want another accident or disappointment, not ever. I want only happiness, health, success, love."

Life did change for her. Life can change for all of us once we rid ourselves of any desire to be sick, or of a sick consciousness. Life and health, success and happiness are bound to come when we build a health consciousness, a success consciousness, a happiness consciousness. One kind is as easy to build as the other. But when we are building our health consciousness we know what we are doing, and we can increase its effectiveness by the fact that we are expecting health and good to come. We are no longer thinking there is any possibility of the not-good. We have the power and the authority to choose health, not sickness. This is one way to decide what we want in our life: Do we want health, or do we want sickness?

Today I choose health. God washes me clean of any desire for anything except health. Gone are all sickness-attracting ideas and attitudes that I have unintentionally acquired.

I do not want to be sick for any reason.
I do not want a sick consciousness.
I want a health consciousness.
I want to be strong and well now and always.
This is what I really want—health!

III
Prevention and Cure

Avoiding illness has always been part of the health picture. How many times have we been told to be careful—careful not to get our feet wet, careful not to sit in drafts, careful not to get close to people who aren't well, careful of what we eat, careful to get the right amount of sleep. Medical science continuously investigates ways to prevent sickness. Immunizations have been developed with prevention in mind; corrective surgery is done to prevent illness. Weight reduction is urged, exercise is encouraged, all as preventive measures. More people today than ever before are trying to eat right, adding vitamins and minerals, getting the purest and best foods they can. More of us are thinking about prevention on the physical side—but we haven't thought much, if at all, about prevention from the spiritual point of view.

In fact, most of us, even if we have been using spiritual methods of healing, haven't thought at all about using our understanding and knowledge of Truth to keep us well. How much easier and happier our lives will be when we can prevent ill health, accidents, all physical problems by using spiritual comprehension and techniques! The wonderful truth is that we can. We can use Truth to prevent as well as to heal discordant conditions. But before we think about prevention we have to think about cause.

What causes illness? What is back of accidents? What causes one person to "catch" and "have" everything going, makes another "accident prone"? What brings our own ill health, even if it is only once every ten years? Medical science is telling us more clearly all the time what metaphysics has always known: our body outpictures and attracts what is inside, and this "inside" includes not only the body but the conscious mind, the subconscious, and the superconscious. Metaphysically, disharmony of body and affairs comes only when we forget who we are: children of God, created to express all the qualities of the Father, including health and harmony in all of our world.

Most of us are aware of our conscious mind all the time. Some of us become aware of the superconscious mind in prayer and meditation. It is the subconscious that has most of us fooled about its activity. The conscious mind deals in the sense world. Through it we recognize objects and persons, learn worldly knowledge, get degrees, licenses, transact business. Perhaps its greatest job is to choose what information is given to the subconscious and make connections for us with our superconsciousness. But even if we are not aware of the working of our subconscious or the superconscious, we can never be separated from either. We need to understand, appreciate, and use all three minds in order to become a whole person.

Our subconscious mind controls all body functions whether we are asleep or awake, aware of them or not: breathing, heart action, circulation, elimination. It is also a storehouse of memory of everything we have ever thought, said, or felt, or have heard other people say. It remembers every wish, every condemnation, every threat. It is the original computer, with unlimited capacity. It is never too full for more data; it is always listening, waiting for more, absorbing at once. It also houses the race consciousness—those ideas and beliefs that come to us through environmental factors, family, other people, national culture, general beliefs, and teachings.

What does our subconscious do with all this hodgepodge of information and emotion? Since it always wants to please us and do what it thinks we want it to do, it makes sure that we experience *what we have said or thought or expressed a desire to experience at some time or other in our life.* It has no judgment, no power of choice; it simply delivers what we have told it to deliver. It never starts anything. It carries things out. This is why psychologists and psychiatrists probe back, back, back, for they know (as we Truth students know) that our subconscious is working under old orders, and will continue to do so until we give it new orders.

Man has always had the power to choose his thoughts and emotional reactions. This is a power of the conscious mind. It is *because* we can choose that we can decide what we put into our subconscious and what we want taken out. This is the way the conscious and the subconscious work together to prevent sickness and to heal body, mind, finances, or relationships. We have much training to do, much cleansing and erasing. Our conscious mind has to stop judging by appearances and know the difference between a present fact and the truth, to look at a sick condition and know that it can be changed, because wholeness is the truth about everything that concerns man. It is through a perfect blending of action between the two that unity with the Father comes about and we start to expand, we open up and let flower our superconscious or Christ consciousness. Prevention of disease of any kind starts with this knowledge that we must and can harness our moods, control our emotions, decide what we think and want. When we do this we are molding our life experiences into the form we want.

Nora accepted this possible way to keep from having a return of illness. She was not as concerned about knowing what had brought several past serious illnesses into her experience as she was in preventing any more. Her prayer was: "*Thank God I am and can be what I think, that I can choose thoughts and desires that will prevent my ever being sick again. Joyously I direct health-filled thoughts and ideas to my subconscious, knowing that it will demonstrate health, strength, healing, energy, vitality, renewal, beauty, youthfulness.*"

As she prayed this and similar prayers, she felt "the power" released in her. Her whole body seemed to come alive as it had never been before. She said that she could see now why her life had been such a physical mess. Her thoughts had been going first this way, then that. Now she was taking control, directing all her thoughts toward health and wholeness. It took her awhile, as it does most of us, to realize fully how powerful our thoughts and words are, and that they are really creators of our life.

Emilie Cady points out that God could have thought and thought the world, but He had to speak the word; He had to say, "Let there be . . . " This is surely what John meant when he wrote, "In the beginning was the Word, and the Word was with God, and the Word was God."

As she understood this more clearly, Nora saw both the possibilities and the opportunity for creating a new life, as well as the responsibility and the possibility of forming what she did not want. To keep her aware, she reminded herself often of Mark's words:

"Therefore I tell you, whatever you ask in prayer, believe that you receive it, and you will."

Yes, through our thinking and speaking we can improve our health. A woman had feet that had become unsightly. She wanted to see if her words to them would help. She had read Myrtle Fillmore's *How I Found Health,* explaining that life is simply a form of energy and has to be guided and directed in man's body by his intelligence, by thinking and by talking. She talked lovingly and encouragingly to every part of her body, and her healing came. So this woman talked to her feet: "*Love is healing you, straightening you, making you beautiful. You no longer hurt. You are smooth and perfect.*"

The skin of her feet did become smoother, softer. Her feet hurt less. The woman persisted, although no other improvement showed. Then one wonderful day she looked at her feet as she started to care for them and she was amazed: the change had come so gradually she had not been aware of it. They still are not the perfect feet she continues to picture, but her feet are no longer ugly and they never hurt.

Charles Fillmore tells us graphically of the power of our words on our body: "Every time we speak we cause the atoms of our body to tremble and change their places." If our words can do this, they can make the cells of our body dance into place, free from any restrictions of negative thinking. It is wonderful to think that nothing in the body is static, that all can be changed with our emotion-packed words of direction to our inner man. Edwin discovered this as he worked to cure the after-effects of a slight stroke and prevent a recurrence. The flesh and muscles on one side of his body were flabby and unresponsive. They were dead-feeling and dead-looking.

Scientists tells us that the body is completely changed periodically. Metaphysically we know that the same conditions persist in the "new" body because the same thought and belief patterns remain with us. Edwin wanted to see if he could so fill his mind with thoughts of body perfection and health that he could create a perfect new body. He kept telling his body that God was in control; he kept telling his subconscious that health was all he wanted and all he would accept. Every morning and every evening he went all over his body from head to feet speaking words of strength and power, healing and love:

"My wonderful body, all is well with you and for you. I love every part of you, I bless every function. You have today [tonight] to refresh yourself, restore, revitalize yourself. I feel strength coming back. Muscles are firming, skin is tightening, glowing. Every bit of you is alive. All is well."

In a few weeks friends were amazed at the change in Edwin's appearance. He was working full time, his muscles were alive, his skin was firm and healthy-looking.

Isaiah holds out this same hope: "You shall be called the repairer . . . the restorer." This passage started Grace Field on the way to relief from apparent bone deterioration and to restoration of strength. She knew that God's power is the only power, but she also knew that she had been thinking there was another power tearing her body down. Realizing the possibility for healing through destroying any belief in anything but God and the power of right ideas and right words, she got busy. She made a number of small signs to put about her apartment: *God is the only power and presence in my body and my life. I am one with God power and this is quick and mighty to heal me now. I do not have to wait; the healing starts immediately.*

Grace particularly liked the thought of the immediacy of God's healing power. It seemed that each of these cards vibrated with an energy that was becoming part of the healing taking place in her body. She made herself keep from looking at the bodily appearance of weakness, and look instead to the permanent health and strength of her spiritual body. At first she felt she had to "turn on the power." Then the wonderful truth came to her that she didn't—that she couldn't—that the power works by itself. Our turning it on is only giving it our attention, our recognition, and our understanding that it is working.

She learned other truths that helped speed her full recovery. Some of them were difficult to accept at first. One was that there is truly nothing for us to heal. All we have to do is accept the possibility of healing, and expect the healing to take place. It took her a little time to learn to look to the healing and away from the body. This is what all of us need to learn.

Two mothers learned this. One had a call from the police informing her that her teen-age son had been badly hurt on his motorcycle. The other had a government notice that her son had been seriously wounded in Vietnam. Both mothers had to look to the healing and not the horror. For both it was a matter of completely controlling their thoughts and emotions, putting their sons in God's care and then not interfering with the healing process by their worry thoughts and imaginative picturings of fearful results. Their statements of healing were similar:

"God in the midst of you is mighty and sure to heal you. Infinite perfection is now working unhindered by me or anybody else in every cell of your body. Whatever needs to be done for you is being done now. Healing is taking place without delay." Both ended their statements with, *"I decree this in the name and through the power of Jesus Christ, Amen."*

Using the Christ power brought home to the consciousness of each mother the fact that Jesus knew He did not do the work but was so at one with the Father that the work was done for and through Him. They knew it would be this way for them. It was not an easy period, but they were diligent in their self-disciplining, and the healings came.

These are ways we can prevent ill health and cure conditions or circumstances. Prevention and healing go together. When we heal we should be starting preventive action; when we prevent, we should be establishing health. We know that God within is the healer, no matter what outer steps we take. We deliberately cleanse our mind and heart of old ideas concerning the inevitability of sickness, or of any possibility of our wanting to be sick. We speak only words of health and healing, and we expect only health and healing.

I no longer expect to be sick.

I refuse to think that anybody has to be sick.

I erase old fears about ill health.

There is no time in my life when I am "bound" to have physical problems or weaknesses.

I am careful about what I think about my body.

I think thoughts of health, strength, beauty, youthfulness, energy.

I speak only words of health and healing.

I picture only health as my inheritance as a child of God.

God in me can prevent sick conditions and God in me can heal.

IV

Healing: Delayed or Incomplete; Instantaneous or Complete

"Why does it take so long? Why can't I get an instantaneous healing? Why isn't everything cleared up? I've been praying a long, long time and nothing seems to be happening. I'm discouraged!"

We've all said such things, asked them, thought them. We wonder about other people who are so faithful in their application of Truth, and yet things don't happen right. We think of Jesus Christ. There was no delay in His healing, no wasted time in getting results. His healings were "right now." That is what we all want: healing now, right now. Sometimes we get a right-now healing. But even if we have an instantaneous healing once, the next time we may not. We wonder why. Sometimes it takes two or three weeks. Sometimes it takes two or three years, sometimes longer. We want to know why, and we should know why.

Why are some healings not only instantaneous but complete? These are the ones we want to know more about. They seem to be so easily come by; they seem to come so effortlessly.

That is part of the answer—the ease, the lack of effort. We don't push and strain when we know how to do a thing; we simply do it. We have to become so practiced in healing that we have a deft sureness comparable to our ability in other things. For some of us this sureness comes quickly; for others it takes longer. We may delay this by trying too hard. "I prayed so hard." "I affirmed so hard." "I denied so hard."

The word *hard* is a good one to eliminate from our vocabulary; we don't want anything hard in our life. We certainly don't want any hard problems, any hard times, and we must not do any hard praying. We should listen to see how often we are using this little four-letter word in places where we shouldn't use it. We know that no burden is heavy with the Father to help carry it; no problem is hard with the Father to help solve it. No times can be hard if we let the Father direct and guide. Praying should not be hard, either, for praying should be the most enjoyable thing we do.

Ordinarily we find ourself praying hard when we are actually arguing with ourself, trying to convince ourself. We have been praying hard if we find ourself tense and tight and not refreshed when we say "Amen."

Are we happy over our prayers? Rita wasn't. In fact, her prayers exhausted her. She needed and wanted a physical healing. She believed a spiritual healing was possible. She couldn't understand why it didn't come; she had had spiritual healings before. Finally she gave up.

"Father, I give this condition to You. Heal it when it is the right time and in the right way. I am releasing the whole mess to You. It's Yours. If You want me to do something about it, tell me. Thank You."

She was so relieved that she felt better. She got out of the way of the healing power, and her healing came very soon. "I'm through with hard praying," she said. "From now on, I'm simply going to take my mental hands off the matter, give it to God, and wait, knowing that He is taking care of things and it doesn't matter when He gets around to doing the work."

Even if we smile at the idea of God with a list of healings to "get around to," the concept of time can be a deterrent to healing.

What difference does it make if we are healed Thursday morning or Wednesday night, March 15 or June 10, if the healing is accomplished? Ten years later, three months later it will be impossible for anyone to remember exactly when the healing came; but all will remember that there *was* a healing, and what was learned and experienced during the healing. If we think of God as everywhere present, without beginning or end, then we know that He doesn't have to pay any attention to time. *God is.* Mary Pickford reportedly said that time was only the noise the clock made—and this is an excellent attitude. The length of time involved is not the important thing; *the healing is*. In Spirit we know we are already healed, so time is incidental. We've been told that a watched pot never boils, that Christmas will come if we forget about it. When we look too closely at time, it crawls; when we don't watch it, it flies. In healings, time can be much the same.

Tom Andrews didn't once think about how long it would take to heal his chest injury, and the healing was almost instantaneous. He doesn't know the moment the healing took place. The important thing was that it happened.

He had been injured when another car approaching the same intersection did not heed a stop sign. Tom had believed to the last second that the other driver saw him and would stop. He was so surprised when the man crashed into him broadside that he didn't believe it. Everything was amicably taken care of by the other driver, the investigating officer, the insurance agent. No, Tom assured everyone, he was not hurt. Later he was very thankful that he had not thought he was hurt.

His wife insisted that he go to bed to rest until a replacement car was delivered to him. It was when Tom turned over in bed that he knew he had been injured. He had felt a little discomfort when he undressed, but as he turned over he was surprised to discover that the two sides of his rib cage had separated. Carefully he lay back; carefully he did what he called "a divine adjustment under guidance." The sharp pain stopped. He said, "Thank God." His wife brought pillows and packed them around him so that even when he was asleep he would not move. He prayed and slept, prayed and slept. One Bible verse never left his consciousness. He thought of it as he went to sleep and it was in his thought when he awakened: "I will restore health to you, and your wounds I will heal."

"Not once did it occur to me I was not being healed," he said later. "Not once did I think there would be any delay, or that healing would take a long time—or *any* length of time. I didn't think that I was doing any big thing. It seemed natural and the easy thing." He stayed in bed two days. The first day he was free from discomfort; the second day "was probably unnecessary." The third day he was up and about his usual activity.

Tom respected his body and didn't do gymnastics or weight-lifting, but he went about his regular routine. He told no one about all this until he remembered, years later, to tell me.

But what if our healings don't come this quickly or completely? When conditions we are praying about do not improve, when needed good does not appear, what do we do? Stop praying? Start praying about something else? In other words, do we give up on the healing we want and need? No, never. This is the time for standing firm, for persisting, for keeping on keeping on, for hanging on to our sureness that the healing is coming regardless of appearances, regardless of the length of time. This is the time to know that no matter how it seems, our good, our healing is at hand. Jesus Christ taught persistence in His story of the man who kept knocking until his friend finally got up and gave him food. Healing will come if we persist.

One woman had a very painful condition that did not respond to medical treatment; later it seemed not to respond to Truth. Finally she decided that since we all believe in the power of the name of Jesus Christ or we wouldn't use His name so often to conclude our prayers, there must be something to it. So she repeated "Jesus Christ" over and over and over for several hours. Her healing came.

A man in his misery heard himself cry out, after all else seemed not to be working, "My God, my God!" The words brought to his mind the agony of the Cross, and he felt he was experiencing a little of what Jesus had experienced. "I didn't add, 'Why hast thou forsaken me?' because I knew that God had never forsaken Jesus Christ. I knew this as I never had before, and it brought me a sense of peace so deep and wonderful that I knew the pain would cease, for my God had not forsaken me either." His pain left while he was contemplating this wonderful assurance of God's presence and help.

A woman used the words: "Loving Father, take care of me now. I feel Your tender loving care." She found this always brought healing of any need. "Sometimes," she said, "the healings tarried, but I persisted."

This is very little for us to do—to persist. Sometimes delay frightens us. Sickness or sick conditions can be frightening, and the fear has to go before the healing can come. Fear constricts, fear represses, fear depresses, fear does not heal. Lois finally realized that it was fear that was holding back her healing. There were plenty of human reasons why she should be afraid. Her condition was considered critical and nothing seemed to be changing the picture.

It seemed to do no good to deny that she was afraid or that there was anything to be fearful about. She realized that her emotions had her bound so tightly that it was no wonder healing couldn't come. She searched her Bible and there she found two passages that relieved her anxiety. Her ill health had popped up suddenly, so Proverbs 3:25 meant much to her: "Do not be afraid of sudden panic." She had been frightened by the sudden fear that the first diagnosis had raised in her. Her confidence in herself returned when she read Psalms 56:3: "When I am afraid, I put my trust in thee." The Psalmist had known what it was to be afraid, as she had been, but he went on trusting God. Had *she* really trusted Him? Was her fear perhaps partly a lack of assurance that He could be trusted to heal her? She made some personal affirmations:

"I trust You, God, no matter how scared I am."

"I do not doubt Your healing power."

"I expect Your healing power to heal me now."

These repeated statements helped bring order to her thinking. They also helped Lois to begin looking toward the healing and away from the threatening. She started to think of herself as whole and well, and not as a sick person.

Another woman told me that she too had a "delayed" healing after she had started thinking of herself as whole. She found that her health was much better as she thought of wholeness and of herself as a health-filled person. For years she had thought of herself as a woman with health problems. Now she no longer thinks of herself as a sick person even if a healing is needed, but a person *ready for a healing!*

"I also got mixed up about who is the healer," she said. "I used to have this feeling of responsibility for doing the healing myself. I thought *I* had to do something to heal me. It took a while for me to realize that I never do the healing. God does. No *person* heals, he only makes it possible for healing to take place."

Sometimes we depend on a friend, minister, counselor, or practitioner to do the right thinking for us and say the healing words. Often we need support, but we need to be very sure we do not think that this other person is doing the healing. All anyone can do is open the door.

Healings are sometimes delayed because we don't listen after prayer. It is in this quiet time that the answer can come. It is then that the inner voice can let us know what we should do. If we don't listen we can miss guidance that would lead us quickly to our healing. Sometimes the things that come to us as we are still after prayer startle us. They may be simple. They may be things we should have thought to do automatically. They may even be seemingly outlandish things.

A very plain-spoken man came to show me his slimmed-down figure. I had heard that he had been ill. No, he said, that had not taken off the weight, but it had started it. He was new in Truth and he was going about it as he did his construction business, with all he had. He had not been sick in years. He didn't think there was any bad feeling inside him against anybody. He didn't hate anyone and he wasn't afraid of anything in the past or present. Then he got sick, very sick.

"I couldn't say anything except, 'God, what'd I do wrong?' Then I got still, to hear what He might have to say, and did I get the surprise of my life! God talks my language. He doesn't pretty things up with big words.

" 'You've been stuffing your gut,' He says. That made me sit up. I was surprised. Now, I could have said that to someone but I expected God to talk differently, big words, nice, you know. When the shock wore off, I knew He was right, as usual. I had been doing exactly that. I always believed it took a whole lot of food for me to do the hard work I do. I stuffed myself all right. I don't any more—and that's where the excess baggage went.

"I take my time eating, and I'm learning to be real choosey about what I put inside me. I'm watching what I think about too. While I was sick I unloaded an awful lot of bad thinking that I didn't know I still had in me. I thought I was 'way past all that, but I didn't let it bother me much. Good riddance, I called it."

"Good riddance" it is for all of us, when we see ourselves for what we are and have been and know that we don't have to be that way anymore, that we don't have to go through unhappy experiences anymore.

Roland called it garbage: "To think I've been carrying all this garbage around with me all these years. It bothered me for a while and then I simply blessed everybody involved, including me. I thought about how differently I would have handled situations, had I known what I know now. I didn't, so I can't change that, but I don't need to carry it around with me—and I do know what to do in similar situations now, so I can avoid a lot because I've been through a lot."

He helped himself come to this realization by using the following statements: *"The love of God is purifying all my past. It is gone out of my life for good. I learn what I can from it and let it go. Both my conscious and my subconscious minds are filled with Truth. I am free from anything in my past or present that is not for my highest good now. I release everybody in my past and present to their highest good. We are all free to be, to do, and to have what God has for us now."*

Once Roland had cleared out all the emotional burdens from the past, his healing came. Many of us do have to rid ourselves of handicapping memories as well as handicapping attitudes and beliefs. When we do, the healing can come, whether it is healing of the body or of our relationships and affairs.

Once we get out of the way, our wonderful body can go about its God-given business of healing. We make it possible for the God power to operate in us and through us. Doctors know that they don't heal their patients. They do all they can to make it possible for the wonderful healing potential in the body, this God power, God nature, to function. The body is equipped to heal. The body wants to heal. We get all our emotional hand-ups, our prejudices, our sick notions out of the way, and our bodies can be healed. We look away from appearances of disease and look to God, do what mystics have termed "abandoning ourself to God." The more completely we abandon ourself to God, the faster and more complete recovery seems to be.

One woman "abandons herself to God" by visualizing the hand of God. Then she mentally writes her request for healing and places it in His hand. Another sees herself in the hand, or sees others she was praying for there. Another sees the hand bringing healing; another feels the hand soothing and healing as it touches.

There are countless ways that we can help bring about healings in our life. It is the natural thing for healing to take place. Healing is already God-provided-for. What we are really learning is to let the healing happen. We can help it happen by knowing where the healing comes from—God—and that we do not have to do the work.

My healing is from God, not from man.
My healing can be now. I do not have to wait.
My healing is complete, for God does the work.
Nothing in my past interferes with my healing.
Healing is not hard work; it is easy; it is sure.
I release my physical problem (or whatever it is) to God. I place it safely in His hand.

V
The Holy Temple: Its Care

Many of us take better care of our pets than we do of ourself. We often abuse our body unmercifully. We expose it to weather conditions, we overwork it, we stuff it, we put abominable combinations of food and drink and drugs into it. We do not keep it in shape. We don't exercise it and then we make it work long hours without rest. If our body weren't made so wonderfully it could never take the use we give it. Religions haven't helped much, either. Too many of them have downgraded the body, even made it a good thing to abuse it.

Penitents crawled on their knees for miles, walked on sharp or hot objects, flagellated themselves. The church has promoted the theory that if the body suffered, the soul profited. Had there been virtue in illness and physical handicaps, Jesus Christ would not have healed—but He did. Healing is necessary and important. Our bodies are important, no matter how we treat them or how they have been considered in the past. Jesus told us why.

He called the body the temple of God. He said that He and the Father were one. If one, then no separation; if one, then one in the same body. Paul told us that God "does not dwell in houses made with hands," and that "God's Spirit dwells in you." If we accept our oneness with the Father, if we believe that He does dwell within us and within all else (and this we must believe if we believe that God is omnipresent), then we will start taking better care of this physical temple, our body. We know God has to express through us. This is another reason why we must keep our mind, body, and emotions as sound and healthy as possible so that we can be a fit channel for Him to express through. It is that simple and it is that important. It is also something most of us have to learn.

We are rather contradictory in our thinking about our body. One moment we think it is fragile, for it can take so little to snap the cord of life; the next moment we consider the body indestructible, for it endures so much. It can take abuse, it can take lack of food, lack of rest, lack of exercise; it can endure savage emotions, frights, exposure. Yes, we are truly marvelously and wonderfully made. We marvel at the human body particularly when we see a baby—so beautifully formed, fingers, toes, skin, eyelashes, everything perfect. No sculptor could approach such perfection. Then we look at our own body and at other people's bodies and we see what we let happen to us.

Lines are on our face from the emotions we allowed; body outlines are lost in a mass of fat that indulgence has accumulated; shoulders are slumped because we do not sit erect. We let so many things happen to the wonderful body we were given. We know what to do about our body. Sometimes we start to take physical care of it. Only as we become completely aware that we are a very special person, God's child, chosen to house the God power, the God nature, the God presence, do we become reverent about our body and want it to be a fit place for the Spirit of God to inhabit.

Merle discovered this, and she found health she had never known. Nothing anyone told her stopped her from abusing her body. She was thin, intense, worked hard. She ate irregularly, she slept irregularly and never enough. As for being outdoors or exercising or relaxing or having fun, there was never time. She used tranquilizers when whe became too tense; she kept herself going with coffee. She kept a candy bar on her desk for a quick energy pickup. Many things went wrong with her body. She had several minor surgical operations. Doctors told her, as friends and family did, "Take care of this body of yours."

Merle laughed and went on. Her body had come through everything; it still would. She was not concerned. Then the truth of the holy temple's location hit her. A bolt of lightning could not have been more shocking. A vision could not have surprised her more.

She was so stunned by the revelation that she had little trouble changing her ways of living. She didn't have to learn what to do; she had been told for years by everyone. It was only the doing that she had to manage. To help, she used these statements many times a day (and always before she went to sleep):

"This body of mine is the temple of the Lord. He is here with me, in me, right now. All I have to do is know He is here, and keep His temple as it should be. It is not only my body, it is His temple. I know what to do to keep it clean, strong, pure, health-filled, perfect. I rest, I sleep, I exercise, I eat proper foods, I drink ample liquids, I keep my body clean, and it becomes more beautiful each day as it responds to my loving care."

Her body responded quickly. Not only was she a different-looking person, she was a different person.

Gone was the person who never had time for recreation or fun. Gone was the tense, demanding perfectionist. Gone was the woman who thought nothing of abusing her body. Instead there was a relaxed, happy, healthy individual.

A harried mother of four little boys found that all her life changed once she learned to respect her body as a temple of the living God. Her responsibilities were around the clock; she had little time to think of herself. Vitamins didn't put color back in her cheeks or a gleam in her eyes. She felt she could not be herself and feel peppy again until the boys were older, when she would not have to do all the physical things she now did. She wasn't unhappy; she didn't resent the boys; she loved her husband; but she was giving her body a beating with a seemingly endless round of what had to be done. All this changed when she got the picture of what she was really doing.

She was not simply hurting herself; she was hurting the holy temple. This was something that could not be put aside until the boys were older. The Father, she knew, was within her and since He was, she must see to it that His temple was a fit dwelling place for Him. It was amazing how her whole life changed once she used statements similar to those Merle used:

"I am the temple of the living God. God dwells in me and I take good care of His temple. My body is wonderful. It is provided for me so wonderfully because it is the temple. I take wonderful care of it. I am renewed in strength and vitality. I am younger than I have ever been because I let God express His life through me. I am more beautiful than I have ever been, for the beauty of God is within me and I let it

express now. I am stronger than I have ever been, for the strength of God is in me now. I am wiser than I have ever been before, for the wisdom of God is within me. I am more loving than I have ever been before, because the love of God is part of me."

She talked about it to her children. The four-year-old "got it" first. She knew he understood when he ran in one afternoon and said, "I want a nap." She was surprised because for, at least a year, he had been fighting afternoon rest so hard that she had given up.

"Why do you want a nap now?" She didn't want it to be a probing question and she didn't want to stop a good idea.

"Oh," he said nonchalantly, "God in me is tired. He says He wants a nap."

Each of us will be like this four-year-old once we accept the fact that our body is God's home, the only place He has to be, and from which He talks to us. We will know what we need to do about all things if we listen to our Guest. We will assuredly know what we need to do to regain, establish, and maintain perfect health. A super race will come when all mankind realizes that every man's body is the dwelling place of the heavenly Father. Yes, every man will recognize his own holy temple and be guided by the Father within, even as Jesus Christ was. We do not have to wait for every man to find this out. We only need to find it out ourself.

We must do more than know it with our mind, more than accept it mentally. We have to know it with our heart and our soul and with all our might. We must *feel* that it is His home. This is the way to show God we love Him, by caring for His home. We all know people who say they love others yet use them terribly; either they do not know what love is, or they only *think* they love. So it is with us. If we love God, we will take care of our body, His holy temple. We will care for our body with love regularly, not for a time and then forget. Our body will sing songs of praise to the Father when we do.

Every temple has its music. Scientists tell us that the cells of our body make music, that they are created by harmony and create harmony when they are healthy. So we listen for the music of our own body. We know that as we keep our cells in harmony or help them restore harmoniously there will be celestial music for the God within, and there will be light.

Every temple should have light, beautiful light. Again scientists tell us the beautiful truth about ourself: there is light at the center of each body cell. These lights, these cells, can be replaced by the wonderful healing power of the body, even as we replaced burned-out electric light bulbs. By helping our body to health, we provide the beautiful light our temple should have, light from perfect cells.

We must do intelligent things for our body. We must keep it clean, exercised, fed, rested, happy. It may not be easy for us to think this highly of our body. We've pushed it aside so long for many reasons. It takes most of us a little time to get to the place where we respect our body and appreciate it. It should be appreciated; it is a wonderful creation. It is more marvelous than man could conceive or plan. We become aware of all of the vital functioning that goes on whether we know about it or not. We don't have to start anything going, we don't have to keep anything going (unless we let disease occur). We don't have to draw a map for the body to follow to circulate the blood. We don't have to set up an irrigation and elimination system. We don't have to make plans for the body to follow to heal a cut, a scratch, a burn, or a broken bone. We don't even have to stay awake to check on the body's working. The more we realize, the more we appreciate.

When we comprehend completely what the holy temple means to us, we help accelerate the healing processes. If we know that the God power is within, at hand, always with us, in us, all around us, it is not difficult to believe that healing can and will come quickly. No matter what kind of healing we want or need, keeping our holy temple as it should be means that we are aware of the God within and thus alert to our healing power. We are part of the power. We can claim it. We can use it. We know that it has to be where the Father is, and the Father is ever with us.

Sometimes this temple is called the secret place of the Most High. It is the place where our three minds—the conscious, subconscious, and superconscious—meet. It is secret because no one can hide there but us; no one else can go there for sustenance, protection, guidance, love, or blessing. And secret, too, because no one can lead us to it. We have to find it ourself. It is a place of realization, understanding, at-one-ment. It is the place where we finally *know* that we are the child of God. It is the place where we really know God, hear God, feel God. It is the place where we have access to all the God-ideas we need to make our life all that it should be. It is the place where we become aware of "my lord and my God." No one else except us can become aware of the God within us.

This is the beautiful wonder of the holy temple. It is sacred, personal, perfect. It is practical, too, for it is where we get whatever we need, whether it is guidance, inspiration, assurance, comfort, strength, or healing. When we listen in our holy temple we are not listening to ourself or thinking our own thoughts, we are listening to the God within us. Nothing can bring greater joy and happiness. So we care for our temple, our body, and the body becomes happy and our life becomes all that it should be.

Truly the Lord is in His holy temple, my body.

Today, now, I know that the Lord is in His temple.

I feel the Father in His temple. I know He is there.

Yes, the Lord is in His holy temple and all is well.

VI
Healing Habits

Sometimes the sickest thing about us is the habits we have allowed to get in control of our life. For once a habit is out of our control, it controls us. It decides what we eat, drink, where we go, how we spend our time, how much work we do, whether we save money or are successful. It's so easy to let a habit get beyond us. We do a thing once; it's that much easier the next time, and the next. Unless we are on the alert, we can find ourself saddled with an unwanted habit that is firmly fixed, and we do all kinds of things either to get rid of it or to pretend it isn't really there.

If it's biting our nails, we avoid looking at our hands. Then we get all dressed up and there we are with those awful-looking fingertips. Maybe it's too much coffee-drinking. In fact, we aren't enjoying food at all or eating what we should. Sometimes we find we've set up some very bad speaking habits. Now and then we hear what we are saying and we realize what we are doing to other people and we don't like the way we feel ourself. Or we listen and we hear ourself using foul language. Oh, there are so many undesirable habits we let get started! Not one of us ever intends letting any of them gain control the way they do.

Jack never thought he would let alcohol get to be habit. But now he needed a drink nearly every morning before he could get going for the day. This scared him a little, but not enough. By lunchtime he had forgotten all about that tiny scare and was ready for a drink before he ate. By five o'clock he had quite forgotten that there could be anything dangerous in stopping in for conversation at the Blue Room. It was only a stop on the way home—but often he didn't get all the way home until midnight or later.

The word *alcoholic* kept coming up in his mind but he kept pushing it back. He refused to think that there was any possibility of his being an alcoholic. He tried to pray about it but, he admitted later, he stopped praying because he didn't want God to stop his drinking. He didn't need anybody to control his drinking. He didn't want anyone interfering with his life, not even God.

There were no scenes at home because somehow Jack, no matter how intoxicated, could still be peaceful. He was aware of his wife's displeasure, of the quiet disdain of his teen-age daughters, but it didn't get to him and he was never ugly—just drunk. Money started opening his eyes. At first he thought it was inflation, higher prices. He complained to his wife one night about what the government was doing to his paycheck.

"Being an alcoholic is the worst thing that has happened to your paycheck," she said. "If you want to have your paycheck go further, stop drinking." Perhaps it was because she hadn't raised her voice to him before that he heard her so clearly this time. "You don't believe it?" she said. "Keep track tomorrow, or right now think what you spent today."

He couldn't remember it all; he remembered enough. "I'm not an alcoholic," he said defiantly as he looked up from the short column of figures.

"If you're not you can stop drinking," she said. "I'm glad it's only a habit. Then you can kick it."

"I will," he said.

Then followed an on-again, off-again period. He tried to change his habitual routine but he couldn't. One day he didn't go out to lunch. He stayed at his desk and prayed. When he went home that night without stopping at the Blue Room, he told his wife he had prayed and nothing happened.

"You're home and you haven't been drinking," she told him. "This is something."

Jack didn't think so. He didn't think God was on speaking terms with him. "Well, get on good terms with your angel," his wife said. "There's always one around."

He found it easier to talk to his angel. Jack told him at the beginning that if the angel didn't know anything about curing the drink habit, he should get with some angels who did, and learn fast. There were days when Jack almost hated that angel. It got so he either felt or saw the angel every time he turned around.

The angel wasn't above snatching Jack by the shoulder as he reached out to take a drink. Sometimes he would pull him back as he was entering the Blue Room and Jack simply couldn't push the door open. Sometimes the angel made it next to impossible for him to raise his glass. Jack spilled a lot of drinks.

It was some time before Jack could see anything funny in it. Then one day he did. "Angel," he said, "you've taken advantage of me. You've practically spoiled drinking for me!" For the moment he had forgotten that was why he had called on the angel to help him.

By the time Jack started to enjoy the angel game,

the habit was well on its way to healing. Jack thought about what he had really been praying with the angel, and made his own affirmations:

"I do not have to do this alone. I have all the help I need to break this drinking habit. I have the help of my angel or anything or anyone else that God thinks will help, or that I need. I am healed completely of all desire to drink. Everything in my life is right again. God, I am glad to be healed!"

Smoking habits can be healed, too. Nell was a beautiful woman who wore beautiful clothes and used exquisite, expensive perfumes. Her husband adored her. Then he quit smoking and her heavy smoking started to bother him. He knew he felt better not smoking. He knew all the things that smoking can do to the body and he didn't want any of them happening to Nell. Besides, for the first time he realized how smoking made his wife smell. This really got to him. His wife laughed at him as she sprayed on some of her delicate fragrance.

She didn't laugh the day he told her he had closed out all of her charge accounts and her checking account. "I'm serious about your not smoking," he said. "There is no sense in your buying beautiful, expensive things and then soaking them in nauseating smoke. I'll keep you covered, but not expensively, as long as you smoke. Cheap perfume, too, when all this is used up. Anything but the cheapest is a loss as long as you smoke."

"I believe you're serious," she said at last.

He was. She went to see their lawyer. He laughed, listened, then laughed again. "My advice is, quit smoking. It won't hurt you to stop. It could save your life. If your husband feels this strongly, why buck it? Surely you can't come up with any good reason for not quitting. Why not quit? You have everything to gain and not a thing to lose. Legally," he started, but she wasn't waiting to hear any more.

First she tried an experiment. She didn't smoke for two days, so she could find out if it was true that her clothes smelled. They did. It seemed everything was against her. Everything she read had something in it about the dangers of smoking. She picked up a religious magazine and in it the writer said that it was difficult to see the face of God through smoke. Then someone as a joke, she thought, told her that only worms ate tobacco leaves naturally. Then she gave up.

"God," she prayed, "everything says 'no' to my smoking. Help me get over it fast so I can stop worrying about it. I need all the help You can give me. I feel all battered and bruised as if the world has been beating on me. Heal my appetite for smoking and heal all my hurts."

She found it helped to think of her smoking habit as a sickness. She believed that sickness could be healed; she wasn't sure about her smoking. "If I were seriously sick, I'd know I could be healed," she said. "I've got to know that about this smoking." Many of us feel the same way about smoking. Heal a cold or even a broken bone, yes; get over the desire and habit of smoking? Well, that's a little different!

Nell used healing statements to keep her mind on the possibility of her healing:

"I am not a slave to any habit. I am free.

"I do not have to smoke. I do not even want to smoke.

"I desire only things that are good for me.

"Thank You for Your help. I could not do it alone."

She did not have to do it alone. When her husband saw that she was seriously trying, he did many things to make it easier. After all, he had undergone such a "habit healing" himself and knew what she was experiencing. When we ask for God's help to heal a habit, we never have to do it alone. Not even when it's a ghastly temper that has to be healed, one such as Pat had.

Pat threw things when she got angry, jumped on things, screamed. It didn't take much to make her angry, either. Her family tried to avoid things that had triggered her temper before, but they couldn't be careful enough. After each outburst, Pat was sick, physically sick, and filled with remorse.

She regretted the many things she had destroyed. Some of them were priceless gifts, many of them were rich in sentimental value, most of them could never be replaced. When she planned to be married, her parents said that if she hadn't told her fiance about her temper, they were going to, because it could ruin her marriage. Pat was incensed. She would never get mad at Bob. Her parents were unmoved. He was too nice, they said, to get hurt by an unreasonable, unpredictable temper.

"What am I going to do, God?" she sobbed that night. "I don't want to hurt Bob and I don't want to endanger this marriage before it happens. What can I do?"

She cried herself to sleep. When she awakened she was exhausted. She felt as she did after one of her tantrums. "Oh, no emotion is worth anything," she said, beating at her pillow. "I've got to do something.

I want to marry Bob. What can I do?"

It seemed there was an answer in her mind. "Only pray, instead of getting mad."

That's what she did. She didn't find it easy, but she found that two affirmations kept her in line:

"I care more for Bob than for my temper.

"God is helping me save my marriage. I refuse to destroy this marriage or anything else ever again."

No, it was not easy; but the healing came.

Mannerisms can be helped. One woman who discovered that she was clearing her throat too often used this: *"I do not do anything that annoys other people or detracts from me. I have no nervous habits. I am at ease all the time. God gives me His peace now."*

A man, who was far too large for his own good, helped cut down his habit of overeating by saying: *"I have no false appetite. I want only what my body needs now. I want only perfect foods for my body. I do not overeat. God is in control of my appetite and my weight."*

A ten-year-old boy had not overcome the habit of wetting the bed. He wanted to be free of this habit. He had tried many times, but this time he wanted to try with God's healing help. He knew that: *"God takes away desire for unnecessary liquids and regulates my body functions so that I never wet the bed. I sleep in a clean, dry bed every night. God always answers prayers. He answers this one."*

Within just a few nights, he had his first free one. Then they came more often, until he and his family actually forgot that there had been a time when his bed had had to be changed more than once each night.

That boy had recognized the need for healing a habit as the others did. He wanted to be healed. He asked for God's help and healing. He expected it, and the healing came.

Most of us have habits that need healing. Some habits interfere with our best and most effective living; others do apparently minor damage—but every one can be healed.

Thank God, I do not have to continue with this habit.

Thank God, I do not have to break this habit alone.

Thank God, I have all the help I need to heal this habit pattern.

Thank God, I know each moment what to do about it.

Thank God, I know what to do in place of it.

Thank God, this habit is gone forever.

Thank God, I am healed right now.

VII
Healing Relationships

When we say, "You make me sick," we may not mean exactly that; but, if we become sick a little later, we'd better remember what we said. Often it is a "who" and not a "what" that makes us sick. We let what people do and say get to us and, because we are perturbed, our body reacts and we are sick. *They* have made us sick. We have let *them* make us sick. Our many human relationships have much to do with whether we are healthy or not. They can make us sick, and they can keep us from getting well.

This is not surprising. We know how our body feels even before we see someone we don't want to see. We can be both physically and emotionally drained after an encounter with some person. It may take us several hours or even a day to get over an unpleasant meeting with someone. We get tired faster and we don't do good work when we have to be with uncongenial people. Undoubtedly most "business ulcers" are not job-pressured but people-pressured. It's very difficult to stay healthy when we are not getting along with members of our family or with our co-workers. Other relationships can be problems for us but it is the family and work relationships we spend most of our time with: they are constantly with us; we can't avoid them. However, it does not have to be a long-time relationship that makes us sick; one contact can undermine health. Whenever we have a physical problem that is not responding to treatment, it is wise to question our relationships for possible trouble.

Usually we know what relationship is making us sick. If we are not getting along with husband or wife or boss, then this is the situation we must heal before we can expect the body condition to clear permanently. If we have a sick relationship we should heal it whether there has been any physical reaction or not. Sometimes we have to spend time thinking about our relationships to find the one (or ones) making us physically ill.

Dorothy was reluctant to think that not getting along with one sister-in-law could have anything at all to do with a chronic health condition that nothing seemed to help. Her doctor was a friend of several years. One day he said, as he shook his head over her complaints about not getting any better, "Dorothy, there has to be something eating at you or you would snap out of this."

Eating at her? What could that mean? He suggested that there might have been a serious disappointment or a deep hurt, or "maybe there's someone who is hard for you to take." This clicked with Dorothy. This could be the relationship that was making her ill. There certainly was one person hard for her to take, a sister-in-law. Dorothy got along with all of her in-laws except this one. She had to be with her often, for the two brothers had a shared business interest. There was no way for Dorothy to get away from the woman. Dorothy had to do something about her reactions, and it was not too difficult once she knew what she had to do.

After prayerful thought, she realized that it was peace both she and her sister-in-law needed. The other woman was always riled up about something. She was always emphatic about everything. Dorothy thought about peace, particularly about Jesus Christ's words, "My peace I give to you." When she meditated, she thought about these words. She said them every time she thought of her sister-in-law. She stopped wasting time hoping the other woman would change, or that she would never have to see her again. Instead she said over and over: *"My peace I give to you. You are at peace. I am at peace. My mind is at peace, my body is at peace. We are at peace whenever we are together."*

She tried to make time for even a brief rest before the two couples were together, and to be sure she had "gathered up her peace and spread it all around the house." While her sister-in-law was in her home, Dorothy tried not to hear all of the indignation she "spouted" and to pour on the peace: *"My peace I give to you,"* she said countless times. As she got ready for the sister-in-law she realized how she used to steel herself whenever there was to be a "confrontation." No wonder her body had responded to the strain of the visits!

The change in herself and the change that became noticeable in the sister-in-law amazed Dorothy. She called what she was doing to heal this relationship her "peace magic." The more Dorothy used her peace statements, the more peace she felt herself, and the more peaceful she was in all her contacts with other people. She discovered that she no longer dreaded the family visits and, while the two women never became close friends, their relationship was far from unpleasant. Dorothy uses her peace magic on everybody these days. "Whether it helps the others or not, it certainly makes me feel different. I hope I'll never let another person make me sick again."

We often let others make us sick. It is always up to us what our reactions are to other people. Just as Dorothy worked for peace for herself first, we must use our own special spiritual "magic" on ourself before we can be successful in working for others. Actually, we don't have to be concerned about the other person in the relationship—only with ourself. Our reactions are what make us sick, not the other person or his actions. We will, of course, want to give everyone the good that we find works for us. But we don't have to be concerned about whether or not the other fellow changes, in order for us to be free from any harmful results from a relationship; we can do something about ourself. Rarely can we do much about the other person; almost never until we have done something first about us. Our spiritual "magic" helps us change our patterns of reaction to people who are "making us sick."

Joyce wasn't sick physically, but she knew she had some sick relationships to heal and she must do it very quickly before they made her business sick. She had a dress shop and had rarely had any trouble with her employees. Often when there were new salesgirls there were a few days of suspicion and jealousy before the new ones settled into what Joyce called her family. This time two new ones seemed to range themselves on one side, against the other employees. It was not friendly competition. When the two weren't actually with customers, one went near the door, the other stayed by the telephone to monopolize the "walk-ins" and the "call-ins."

Joyce talked to them. Not about their actions, but about their experience, their backgrounds. She discovered that they were what she called "youth militants," militant about being under twenty-five. She didn't react or say anything when they suggested that she get rid of the "old bags" she had so she could have a "swinging store." The new girls had a lot of ideas for her, many of them were good. She suspected that they thought *she* was too old too! She prayed: "Father, what do I do now? What can I do? You'll have to show me."

All that day Joyce said to herself and thought to herself: "*My Father is showing me how to make this store happy again. His healing love is at work right now. He will tell me what to do at the right time so that everyone will be happy, successful, prosperous.*"

It was a very busy day. By the end of the afternoon Joyce forgot all about this store "sickness." She loved people and she loved to help women find clothes that made them look their best. She went back to the stockroom for a customer. As she stepped through the doorway, she felt as if she had stepped into something heavy, thick, black, ugly. The room was filled with it. One of the new young women was talking through almost closed lips to one of the older employees. Hearing Joyce, she stopped, turned and walked out. With her went most of the bad feeling, but not all of it. Before Joyce could say anything, the other woman left too. The heavy feeling of the room was gone. The two had taken their ugly feelings with them. It had been such a real hate that Joyce was frightened. *What could one do about hate like this?*

The answer came: "Love more than the hate."

The older employee stopped at Joyce's desk before leaving and said she was quitting. Quickly

Joyce said: "We don't make decisions this time of day. Come in a little late tomorrow. We've all been busy today." The young woman who had been in the stockroom stopped too: "Let her go. Your business will be better off without her." Joyce didn't say anything.

Joyce stayed at the store a long time after the others were gone. She refused to remember the hate-filled stockroom. She tried to feel that her store was filled with love, that love was with each one of her employees in their homes, that love was in charge of all their lives and activities. There must be understanding, respect for each other in her store, and wisdom. God had to be in charge of all of them and of everything. She made three strong affirmations that she prayed, meditated about, declared all through the night:

"God is in charge of this store, not me.

"God is healing all bad feelings in this store now.

"We all work for God, not for ourselves, and we are all happy, successful, and prosperous."

God did take charge; the store changed—not all at once, but it changed. Joyce was grateful for each indication of improvement. She knew the victory was God's for sure when one of the new girls left for a better job—and really didn't want to go! "I don't understand it," she told Joyce. "I even like the old . . . no, I can't call them that. They're wonderful people. And you, well, you're groovey!"

We can learn much from Joyce. Not only did she help heal a discordant situation but she recognized the "sickness" before it had gone too far. We should be alert to contacts with people who are unpleasant and very alert to our reactions to them. Sometimes it seems we get dropped into the middle of a very sick situation. If we are, we must avoid "catching" what the others may be taking from each other.

Garland found such a situation when he was transferred to a large office in his company. It was a mess of rivalry, backbiting, politicking. He had been through this before; it had taken a spiritual healing of high blood pressure to teach him to watch his relationships. Because he refused to "play" the way the others did, he was considered strange at first. Garland did not let this bother him. He kept on with the affirmations he had started to use again:

"None of us needs to compete against each other. None of us needs to be afraid of each other. There is plenty of success and recognition to go around for all of us. We are all nice people, and we get along with God's help and guidance."

Two little ideas came to him that made a big difference in the office. He started some fun games during coffee-break times, and a lot of personal rivalry was played off. Then he found out when birthdays were coming up, and the men found it was difficult to be mad when a bunch of them were singing "Happy Birthday." Over the weeks the office relationships healed and there were many benefits. There was practically no absenteeism from illness, business increased, the office won company honors. Several men were promoted and transferred into higher managerial positions. Healing had come. Sometimes when we learn how to heal, we find ourself in situations where we must use what we have learned. Freely have we been given, freely we must share. As we do we are protected from any new, sick relationships.

Healing can come in every type of relationship—even in wife/mother-in-law "sickness." Nothing Ruth could do pleased her demanding, complaining mother-in-law who continued to think of her son as a little boy and the only one who mattered. At first Ruth had been afraid of her, then she resented her, then she hated her. By then Ruth was sick and didn't know what caused it. When she thought of the possibility that the relationship with her mother-in-law was the cause, she didn't know how she could ever heal it, because it had been bad for so long. Ruth was sure that nothing she might do or say would change her mother-in-law. She was relieved when she realized that healing relationships really has nothing to do with changing people—only with changing our attitudes toward them and ourself. Ruth did not see how she could think any differently about her mother-in-law. "I'll have to work on me first," she said.

She remembered that the length of time a physical condition had existed, and the severity of the affliction, never deterred Jesus Christ. The man who had been waiting at the pool for a healing for thirty-eight years and the woman who had an issue of blood for eighteen years were both healed. The healing Christ power had worked every time. She wanted it to heal her now:

"The healing power of the Christ is at work in my mind and body healing me now. The healing power of the Christ is at work in this situation with my mother-in-law now, healing it. A good relationship is now established between us and maintained with God's help. I no longer fear her or hate her. All is well between us now."

Ruth's health started to improve, slowly but surely. Feelings eased between her and her mother-in-law. There were fewer demands and much less criticism. It wasn't fast and it wasn't easy, but Ruth stayed with her resolve not to let anything she thought about her mother-in-law make her sick. As she persisted in her prayers a good relationship did start developing for the two women who loved the same man.

Angie discovered that the relationship she needed to heal was her relationship with God. She and God, as she said, had developed a strained relationship. There was an emptiness in her life that nothing else filled. She had first one thing wrong with her physically, then another. Finally she knew the reason: God was being left out and she was not on "speaking terms" with Him.

"God, I'm ready to be friends again. I've missed You. I can't get along without You. I want You back in my life right now. I'll keep in communication from now on. I need You and I want You."

As in all our relationships, in our closeness with God we have to keep in communication. No relationship stays alive and active if there isn't communication on a regular basis. Angie felt a little awkward at first, as we are likely to feel when we start being with a friend again after an interval of separation. Then she forgot all about her awkwardness: she was feeling better physically. She was happier too. And she regained the easy intimacy she once had with the Father within.

The healing power of the God nature always works when it is invited and allowed to work. No relationship can be so sick that the healing power of the Christ is unable to heal it. It doesn't matter at all who is making us sick; we can be healed. The relationship can become what it always should have been.

Thank God, all relationships can be healed.

If people make me sick, I can be healed and they will never make me sick again.

I take the peace of Jesus Christ into all my relationships.

I am at peace with all people now.

I have no sick relationships; they are all healed.

VIII
Healing Memories

It usually takes a psychiatrist more than one session to diagnose his patient's ills, to find out what is buried in the subconscious and causing present difficulties. Symptoms never tell the whole story. Many things indicate problems. Students tell much more than they plan to say in themes and examination papers. Children reveal a lot in their play talk. Adults say more than their words in idle conversation, if anyone is really listening.

Many of us try to conduct our own investigations and self-diagnoses. Self-quizzes are fun and can tell us things. But it is our memory we need to search diligently through to find out if there is a need for healing. A familiar song says that memories "bless and burn." Memories that bless are not troublemakers; the burning memories are those that leave scars and scar tissue to cause difficulty, sometimes all through our life.

Unlike surface burns and cuts, memory wounds are not visible and, even when we know that an experience has been difficult or painful, we don't always realize the extent of damage done. When we are children, we don't know how to do anything about unhappy events; as we get older, we try to "get over" unhappiness. We do this in different ways. We may try to forget it completely, try to do something to compensate, plan to get even. Rarely are we able to dismiss the happening, learning what we can from it, blessing it and going on without loss of emotion or emotional reaction time. We don't actually put it into our memory. What we do put there (for something of all experiences is stored) is put there without any emotions attached to it—and it is the emotional part of a memory that makes it either bless or burn.

I knew one man who could dismiss happenings. When people acted in ways they shouldn't have around him or to him, he could dismiss them and the situation and say without the slightest bit of rancor, "Well, jolly good luck to you!" He meant it. He held no hard feelings about whatever had happened. He sent the people on their way out of his life and kept no hurting emotions in his memory. He was through with the whole affair.

Too often the way we try to get rid of unpleasantness is like trying to stuff a balloon into a too-small drawer. Part of the balloon keeps bulging out somewhere as we push on another place. Healing the memory is the only way to take care of situations we have allowed to stay in our memory unhappily. Memories that burn, fester. The festering can take outer form as illness, lack, unhappiness, unpleasant personality traits, all kinds of undesirable things.

My first introduction to memory healing as spiritual healing therapy came through a lecture on the subject given by Agnes Sanford, the noted Episcopalian leader in that church's faith-healing program. She found that stubborn conditions that could not be healed otherwise responded to this healing of the memories. It had proved to be a successful healing method for her. It has helped many people I know. Mrs. Sanford had her patients start back from birthdays; this is only a suggestion. We can start thinking of Christmases past, school years, a wedding, the birth of a brother or sister, any point of time. Our search for a bothersome memory may take some time because our subconscious, keeper of our storehouse of memories, is a master in camouflage and cover-up. It has a fetish about saving face for us. It wants to keep us from facing any unpleasantness about ourself, although it has no compunction whatsoever about making us suffer for what it has stored away! It works overtime keeping the conscious mind from knowing what is really going on "down under." It changes, pretties up, our desires and reactions, all our emotions. Even in our dreams, symbolism (instead of our actual desires) comes through to form our nighttime movies-in-bed.

If we have a healing problem or any kind of inharmonious condition that persists despite sincere effort to get rid of it, then we should give memory healing a trial. We are usually in for some surprises when we start asking our subconscious to bring up memories. Some memories surprise us; even though we remember the hurt, we have matured sufficiently to see how ridiculous it was to react as we did. Some memories will be a joy. Some will amuse us, but some will be ugly. Some will be so bad that we will wish we hadn't started to remember. But the more we remember, the surer we are healing is the proper course. While we can generalize our healing-memory prayers, we get better results when we search out a troublesome memory and take care of it specifically.

A woman was going through a trying time when it seemed that everything was keeping her from doing what she wanted to do, no matter how small a desire she might have. Many new responsibilities came to her, many disappointments. She didn't even have any time or place to be by herself to "go back in time." There were always people around her at home and at the office, and she was in a car pool both on weekdays and on Sundays. She was even sharing her bedroom temporarily! She discovered that she did not need a lot of time. She simply seized every opportunity for a minute or two. (A busy mind can cover a lot of ground and a lot of time in a few seconds!)

One evening it was raining when she came home from work. The rain got heavier and heavier. The rest of the family was delayed. At first she was worried, and then she saw this as a chance to be by herself. Before this her mind hadn't summoned any new memories for her recall. Now one came: all of a sudden it was as if she were back on her grandfather's farm. It was raining hard. She had been left alone while the grown-ups had gone to town. The wind started to blow, hard. A tree fell across the steps of the screened-in porch where she was playing. The wind slammed the front door of the house shut behind her. She was trapped. It was a long time before her family returned because of the water on the roads. The feeling of helplessness she had, the terror she felt, all kinds of emotional reactions were remembered—and they seemed a parallel to what she had experienced so often: a feeling of helplessness and of being trapped by responsibility, trapped by people. She kept the word *trapped* in the denials and affirmations that helped her become free from the long-held feeling that she was not master of her life.

"I am not trapped by an condition, circumstance, or person. Nothing, no thing and no person, decides what is to be in my life. God does. God and God

alone directs my life. I am free, free to be all that God wants me to be. No memory interferes at all with my good. All memories that in any way hurt me are dissolved by the Father."

Many other memories came back to her conscious recollection. She was glad for each one, even for the unhappy ones that brought back a flood of other unhappy memories. She continued to use her memory statements and things improved in her life. When she stopped thinking she was always trapped (and it was easier to do this after she remembered the childhood experience), she stopped feeling trapped. Some people dropped from her immediate life; the person who had been sharing her bedroom left; a few responsibilities were lifted. Everything looked and was better.

When we remember unhappy things, perhaps incidents in which we have not played a role we now approve of, we must not let this depress us. What we were then, what we did, the reasons and motivations we had for our actions, are not true of us now. We do not need to be either afraid or ashamed of the emotions we uncover, the fears, hates, or resentments. We need not be affected by these old feelings and events any longer. When a dream comes up in recall we can toss it out forever, so far as its having any power over us or directing any of our actions. We can say: "*Thank You, Father, for uncovering this memory. Thank You for healing any hurt it has caused. Thank You for helping me learn from it and go on to be the happy, fine person I am supposed to be, doing the prosperous, successful things I should. This memory has no more power in my life now or ever. I have grown past it."*

A salesman who had a large area to travel seemed to attract only trouble. Customers often changed their minds. Orders frequently were refused on delivery. Many customers quibbled over bills, claiming prices were not as they expected. The salesman had tried to give honest and right action with good service; he expected the same from his customers. He was careful to speak clearly, to write out orders legibly. He prayed about it. He learned about memory healing, and he was curious.

He took two days off to try healing his memories. He checked into a motel where he had never stayed and asked not to be disturbed. He prayed for guidance and knowledge. He thought back as far as he could; he thought about his parents, his brother and sister, his wife, their children. He even thought about his schoolteachers, as many of them as he could remember. He remembered a lot of things, but nothing that seemed consequential. He decided to go for a walk.

He walked a long way, and came to a school where children were playing. Swings were full, slides were full, the bars were all in use. As he watched, a boy who had been playing on a slide came over to the swing area. He asked for a turn on the swing. No one offered to give up a swing. Then another boy told him in a loud voice to go back where he had been; a scuffle started. The boy in the swing pulled back to start swinging again. The other boy moved, but not fast enough. The boy in the swing slipped, lunged out of the swing, fell, hit his head on the ground, and twisted his leg under him. Blood spurted from his forehead.

"He's hurt! You did it!" the children started calling to the boy who had wanted a swing. "You pushed him!"

"I didn't," the boy yelled. "I didn't! He fell all by himself."

"You pushed me!" the boy who was hurt screamed. "You pushed me! You made me fall. You did too!"

As the salesman walked quickly over to the boys, the words repeated in his mind: "You did. You did. You did." He was back on another playground; there was snow. Children were playing with sleds. He wanted to ride on a big new sled but the older boy wouldn't let him. Then the other boy slipped on the crusty snow and fell, tipping the sled over so that he fell against the end of one of the runners. His face was cut. The other children came running, crying: "You pushed him! You made him fall!" The teachers thought it was his fault, and blamed him for it.

He remembered how the boy's face looked as the cut healed. He remembered his mother saying: "If you did it, say so. People will never like you, never trust you if you don't tell the truth. Everyone says you pushed him. Don't you want people to believe you?"

That was a long time ago. He could do something for this boy on this playground now. "I'll take you inside," he told the boy who was hurt. He carefully put his handkerchief over the scraped places on the boy's forehead. Then he turned to the children. "He's all right. You didn't push him," he said to the boy who was standing off by himself. "I saw it all. You kids know he didn't. This boy's going to be all right. All of you start sharing the swings and everything and stop blaming people for things they didn't do. The boy slipped in the swing. He wasn't pushed. I saw."

The salesman felt better. This boy wouldn't have with him what *he* evidently had been carrying all these years: a feeling of injustice coupled with the belief that nobody would ever believe him.

"People believe me now, Father, they do. They know I give good service and am honest in every way. What happened long ago no longer has any power over me. Any hurt from this memory is healed right now."

Customers didn't change overnight, but the salesman knew that he would have customers who believed him completely. His business did improve; the annoying disappointments ended. He felt free, his own man, as he never had before.

It's no fun not being one's own man; it's no fun being in bondage to anything, even to a memory. The past should be over and done. We should learn what we need and go on. We should not hold to the hurts and disappointments and wrongs of the past. Healing our memories is one way to freedom from things that have hurt us long ago. It is never enough to know what hurts us or keeps us from success and happiness; we have to know what to do about it. When we heal the memory we are not only getting rid of the memory's power to hurt but we are also repairing the damage it has done and protecting ourself from any possible further injury from it.

No memory is so deep, so intense that it cannot be healed completely. No memory can interfere with our good once we have uncovered it. We can release the past and not keep any of the hurt from it. Even memories of doing things that were wrong can be healed, so that only the good we have learned to do remains. Shock can be healed. Betrayal can be forgotten and the hurt healed. When we heal memories we heal conditions in the present and insure healthier, better futures. We can help prevent unhappy memories being stored in our subconscious, too, for we don't want any more unhappy memories around to interfere with our well-being.

We can be grateful for our good memories, for the ability to have our experiences stored; but we can direct our subconscious to store only good, helpful, happy memories: "*Store nothing that can ever be harmful to me again. I want to store only good memories, memories that will help, not hinder me. Retain only the good from every experience I have. I want to select only the good to keep. Thank you for keeping my good, happy, helpful memories for me.*"

Yes, we can take care of memories past and memories present.

God is healing all memories that need healing.
No memory harms me now.
I have only good, helpful memories now.

IX
Healing Failure

Failure can make us sick, and we can be sick of our failures. Failure can be unexpected and sudden, it can be anticipated, or it can be chronic. Sometimes it can seem to be congenital. No matter how failure comes or how we diagnose its causes, it must be healed—and it can be. And the faster we get at its healing, the better for everyone concerned. None of us wants to be a failure at anything at any time. This is good, because the wonderful truth about us is that we do not have to be failures. If we seem to be we can expect a healing in the achievement area of our life. One happy thing about deciding that our failure or failures can be healed is that the very moment we decide a healing is possible, our failures start separating from us.

Sometimes it seems that we like to hug our failures to us. We do this partly because we are protecting them. We think we are hiding them from the eyes of other people. It's bad enough to fail, but it's worse to have everyone know that we have failed. So we hover over our failures. It helps us to let loose of them, to get them out where we can look at them and examine them. Sometimes our failures are so much a part of us that it is difficult to separate ourself from them long enough to study them, to know that they can be healed.

It took Morgan some time to start healing his failure. He had lived with it so long. It seemed that he had failed at everything important in his life. He was a benchwarmer, he thought. When he was a little boy he was always the last one chosen to play. In high school he barely made the second team. College seemed necessary if anyone wanted to be a success, but Morgan didn't get to go to college, and he didn't get to marry the girl he thought he loved the most. Not that his wife was a "second best," but she *had* been second on his list. He hadn't made her life wonderful, what with his not making a go of things even when he inherited some money. That should have made the difference, should have made him a success. But it didn't.

Probably he got in too big a hurry. He hadn't taken time before he made his investments. Almost overnight, it seemed, the money was all gone and everything was the way it had been before. He was simply a failure. Where were all the dreams he'd dreamed all through the years? Morgan was bitter about himself. Then he heard about this idea of healing failure.

Morgan believed in healing in a lot of things, but not when it came to failure. He thought about it a lot—at the office, while he was driving, at home when he was working in the yard. He knew he needed to know more about his failures before he could heal them.

One night he sat up late making a list of all the failures he could remember. Then he sat and looked at the list, a little amazed. He knew he had been a failure but he didn't think he had been such a complete one! He looked at the list a long time before he burned it in an ashtray. Then he tried to make a list of things he could do successfully.

He tried to think what made him happiest. It was a long time before he could write down anything, and then he was surprised at what it was: he was happiest when he did some little thing for somebody. He liked sharpening the neighbor's hedge clippers, he liked helping him transplant rosebushes, he liked making little gadgets for his wife in his workshop, he liked saving time and effort for other people at the office. He could fix a lot of little things for which other people had to call in a repairman. Morgan breathed a deep sigh as he thought about the small talent he had. He thought about the parable of the talents, and he remembered what happened to the man who had only one talent and hid it. Maybe doing for others was *his* only talent. He certainly didn't want to hide it and then have it taken from him, so he set about doing more little things for other people.

"If this is my talent, God, help me develop it," he prayed. And he found a lot of things he could do for other people, more than he ever had done before. He was happier than he had ever been.

It surprised him how much better everything seemed. Even the children seemed to behave better, and his wife, who had always been a "plain" cook, started fixing really special meals. A lot of things were better. At least, he was making more people happy all the time. It shouldn't have surprised him, a few months later, when success started coming to him. The top man in his office asked him out to lunch one day. Morgan liked the restaurant where they went, he liked the food and the service, and he said so.

"You like a lot of things," the manager said to him as they waited for their dessert to be served.

Morgan nodded. Then the manager outlined a job he thought Morgan could do for the company: to be a kind of contact man. He was to call on people whenever the need arose, talk to them, find out what their problems were in relation to the products they were using from the company. The manager said he knew Morgan would be a success because people always like people who like them, and that was all it took.

Henry's healing of failure came in quite a different way. His first marriage hadn't lasted; he had had twenty-three jobs in less than fifteen years. He could always get a job, but he couldn't keep one. There was nothing permanently good in his life; the only thing permanent was failure. His second marriage was on the rocks. Everything looked sick.

Henry knew that many people have healed their physical conditions by staying with the Presence of God, or the Christ. This was the method he chose to try to heal his long list of failures. He visualized the Christ with him day and night. It took a lot of mental effort to do this; however, he had nothing to lose by trying. He was out of a job again, too. Finding a job was never hard. "There's always somebody," he said, "who won't give up on me."

At first it was all pretense with Henry; then something happened. He was no longer simply saying that the Presence was with him, he was no longer trying to feel the Presence—the Presence was there. It was real. It was with him when he went to sleep and he felt It before he opened his eyes in the morning. It even woke him up every morning in time to get to work on time. The Presence seemed to help Henry do a lot of things: he was never absent, he never left at the end of the day without his work completed, he got a lot of good ideas and used them. In less than six months on the new job he had had two raises and one small promotion. His marriage was better, too. Debts had been cut down. Keeping the Presence with him had certainly healed Henry's long-time failures.

George took Jesus Christ seriously when He said again and again that He did not do the works, but the Father. George was tired of failing and of not having things right in his life. His failure seemed to spill over into every part of his life. His business was in a precarious situation, his health wasn't good, his wife was threatening to leave him, he looked at least ten years older than he was. Then everything broke around him: he lost the business, his home mortgage was foreclosed, his better car was taken back, he owed money all over town, his wife took the children and left. He did not blame anyone except himself. But George was tired of failing. If there was any way possible for his failure to be healed, he would try it.

When he started thinking about the healing power of the Father, he got a jolt. If the Father was the one to do the work as the Christ had said, then George didn't have the responsibility for his success or failure any more. He had never felt that he could blame anyone except himself; he had never thought that anyone except himself would make him a success. But if he started thinking and letting the Father do the work in him, this took the load of responsibility from him. He would no longer have to make the decisions, the Father would. George's part would be carrying out whatever the Father wanted done. It was frightening as well as exciting.

"Funny," he said later, "I never once felt as if I was being sacrilegious in talking so with the Father, and neither did I feel religious or pious." As he got into the habit of saying, "Not I, but the Father," he found that he was doing what he should all the time. He found parking places during busy hours; he found people in when it didn't seem logical; if he left the house early, it was right that he did; if he left later than usual, there was always a good reason for that.

Somewhere along the way, as he said over and over, "The Father does the work, makes the decisions, heals my failures for me," George lost the conviction that he was a failure, that life had "ganged up" on him, that he would never amount to anything. "I didn't have to be concerned, because my success was my Father's business, not mine."

Dale was another man who thought the world was against him. It must be, else he surely would have found some way to success before this. Dale was a plodder, a dependable plodder. Inside he was a dreamer, a man who had dreamed a long time about success—but each year the dreams became smaller, fainter.

The business Dale worked for was as dependable and plodding as he was. Business practices were the same as they had been when Dale started working there part-time, eighteen years ago. The same family owned it all; displays of merchandise never varied. There were a few changes, a few improvements, but even one who had not been in the store for a long time could find what he wanted without asking. Dale felt like anything but a success. When he learned of the possibility of changing his dull life of failure, he wanted to try it.

When he started to think success and not failure, his dreams began again. Dale decided that if he was really the son of God, then he ought to be successful. He wasn't used to thinking of himself either as a son of God or as successful. But he liked to think about these two possibilities. Affirmations helped Dale not only to accept the new ideas mentally but to feel that they were true:

"*I am the successful son of God.*

"*I am one with the Father and I do what He tells me to do; I am successful in all that I do.*

"*I am the wealthy, healthy, happy, wonderful, successful son of God.*

"*I am successful.*

"*I do not have to wait any longer for success. My success is here right now, and I am grateful.*"

At first the only change he could detect was that he was happier. Then some good things happened. The store he worked in was sold. The new manager wanted him to be his assistant, with the thought of becoming manager very soon, as the company had many expansion plans. Dale found he had a lot of ideas that had been lying idle in his mind. He was making more money, he liked his work a lot more, he had a future in sight for the first time. His failure was healed.

A man who had had business disappointments allowed them to end nearly all his activity. Various physical ailments developed as he mentally and emotionally crumpled under the weight of disappointment. After trying to heal the body without success, he too tried to heal the failure. That healing came, and so did physical healing. A woman who had not been a successful wife found that with God's help she could be all the good things she wanted to be, to and for her family. Students have found school failures did not have to be repeated but could be healed. Success *is* possible for us, in spite of failure past or present. Our failures can be healed!

Success is my inheritance from my heavenly Father. I am not born to fail but to succeed, and I can.

God's healing power works in all parts of my life.

God's guidance directs my every word and action. I know what to do to achieve success.

I think success. I dream success. I speak success. God helps me bring about success now.

X
Healing Finances

Sometimes our billfolds and bank accounts are undernourished. We can have "sick" pocketbooks. We speak of an unexpected gift or bonus, an increase in pay, as "making us well," and we mean well financially, not physically. We do think about our finances as having "health" or "sickness" possibility. We don't always think that there is much we can do about changing that "health" condition, and we don't always know how to keep our finances healthy. But we can. We need to start speaking words of health (and not sickness) about our financial condition. Sometimes we are not aware that we are using our powerful creative word to keep our money sick. If we think "sick" money, lack, and feel sick about our financial affairs, our subconscious picks up these words and helps us bring about more of the same. To get well and stay well financially we have to start with the way we are looking at our finances and how we are talking and feeling about them.

Jim Bowen had much to change in his financial vocabulary and thinking. He had not realized that he was talking about his money as sick. It seemed that he never had anything good to say about his money or about money in general. He thought his income was too small; when he looked at his paycheck he only saw how little it was. At the same time he thought of all expenses as big and high. At first he thought it was impossible that thinking and speaking thankfully and with praise to the Father could make his paycheck do any more than it had. He was willing, however, to give it a try.

When he got his paycheck the next payday, he made himself sit for a few minutes and look at it, thinking not only that it was a large check but that it was amazingly large, because it could do so many good things for him and his family. Jim had to work on his imagination for a while before he could do this successfully, but he persisted. He made himself think of everything the check would pay for: rent, food, clothing, gasoline, a short trip. He thought of the check as coming not from his employers but from God. He tried to see it as manifestation *for him* of God's rich substance. He looked at the check and mentally increased the numbers on it. He doubled the amount of his pay; he tripled it: he saw it increasing ten times. He thought again of what he would use the money for, and he saw that check covering twice as many expenses as usual, three times as many, ten times as many.

When he paid for anything, whether it was a sack of groceries or a newspaper, Jim remembered to be thankful that he had plenty of money and could afford to buy everything he needed. He asked God's guidance in making wise, appropriate selections. When he paid his bills, he blessed his creditors and thanked them mentally for having trusted him. He thanked them for thinking that he was rich enough, would have enough money to pay. He was grateful that other people were convinced that he had the ability to pay his bills.

Jim realized for the first time that credit is one kind of wealth. He had not appreciated it before. He had felt he had to have credit because he could not pay cash. Now he thought of credit as proving that he *did* have the ability to pay. It made a big difference. Often we are richer than we think; Jim was finding this true. These affirmations helped him:

"*I have a healthy income now. It provides all my needs. My bank account is healthy. It grows and grows and grows. My heavenly Father gives me money for all my needs and wants and tells me how to use it wisely. I enjoy my money now. I bless it. I eagerly watch it increase. New sources of income provide more money for me to use and enjoy. Money comes to me in large amounts in both expected and unexpected ways. I thank God all day long for the great wealth He is giving me now. I am rich, not poor. I am God's rich child.*"

At the end of the month, when the bank returned his canceled checks, Jim looked with happy wonder at them. He felt rich for having written so many checks, not poorer for having so many. This helped him get into the way of thinking that as God's child he had unlimited resources of wealth. Jim found that his present income went further as he appreciated what he had, gave thanks for it, blessed it, and spoke highly of it. He made better use of his income, and with prosperous thinking, ideas for new ways of adding to his income came to him. Jim never referred to his money as being insufficient again; he never spoke about being sick financially. He was healed.

Art had arrived at the financial spot where something had to be done to heal his affairs. His financial condition was critical. For several years he had been slipping deeper and deeper into debt. It wasn't that he was extravagant; some of the expenditures could have been avoided, but most of them were not for luxuries. But Art continued spending a little more money here and a little more money there—a little more than his paychecks would cover. He said money was always on his mind, but this was not true: it was lack of money that was never far from his conscious thoughts, no matter how busy he might be on the job. He learned the truth of the statement that what we give our attention to grows and multiplies. What we take our attention from dies. Art gave his debts all his attention, and they grew and grew.

He had exhausted his credit at the bank. The loan officer was sympathetic. He suggested that Art sell his home and buy a smaller place, or sell his car if he had good bus service near his home or if he could get into a car pool. Perhaps his wife could get a job. Art thanked him. He had tried to work out all of these suggestions before.

House costs had risen since Art and his wife started to buy their home. They found that if they sold their home, that would not improve their situation. They would have to make larger payments on a smaller and less desirable home, and would end up spending more and having less to show for their money. The city bus did not come near their home. As to car pools, Art dropped off their two children and a neighbor's two in the morning, and the neighbor picked up the four children in the afternoon. They had explored the possibility of Jean working. There were two preschool children who would be home for three more years; paying babysitters or nurseries would not leave much from Jean's paycheck. Besides, she was an economical housekeeper; they would be in worse financial condition, Art knew, if it weren't for all she managed.

Then it was suggested that Art needed to change

his mind if he wanted to change and heal his finances. Change his mind? What he was facing was a whole stack of facts of life: regular monthly expenses, so much income, so many bills. But healing always starts in our thinking and this is what Art learned.

He did a number of little things that helped him keep healthy-minded about his money situation. They helped him keep his thoughts centered on freedom from debt and lack and worry, and on plenty.

He made a short list of what he owed. He blessed the bills and put them into a drawer and closed it, saying that he would open it again when they were all paid. The short list looked much more possible than the stack of bills had. He thanked God for helping him pay each bill without delay and without worry on his part. He thought about writing a note to each creditor; then he decided to call. He told the bookkeeper, credit manager, or owner of each business that he had let himself get into a financial bind but was on his way out now, and all creditors would have their money.

The first time he said this he felt he was lying. He added the words "with God's help" to himself, and this made him feel better. Without God's help, Art knew he would never be able to do it. The calls were hard for Art to make; no one likes to say he has got himself into a mess. But the calls did make him feel better. Each payday he paid something to each creditor. Sometimes it was a very small payment, but he never forgot to write a "thank you" and each payday he made a new listing of amounts owed.

He spent extra time with his Bible, looking up references to protection and wealth. He was amazed at the wealth of the early Israelites. Abraham, Isaac, Lot, Jacob were all wealthy men. Then he came to Joseph. Here was a man who had been sold into slavery, and then had made good; he was thrown into prison on a false charge, and came out a greater success than he ever could have been before. Not only did Joseph have riches for himself, he helped his country to get through a difficult period. He also saved many other people, including his own family and the brothers who had wanted to kill him. Art marveled that Joseph kept free from resentment and hurt feelings.

Somehow Joseph talked to Art. It was as if he said: "Art, forget what has happened. Get going now. Don't resent the fact that other people stay out of debt or have been more successful. Learn from this. I made it under rough conditions. So can you!"

Thinking about and studying Joseph's life made Art feel better, encouraged him. Whenever he felt a little down, he thought about Joseph. He also thought a lot about all the wealth of Joseph's ancestors: the thousands of sheep, the gold, the jewels, the fine clothing. All of these men had problems they brought on themselves. All of them kept their faith in God, all of them tithed, all of them prospered. The thought of tithing gave Art more to think about.

He wanted to be able to tithe; he believed in tithing, but he didn't see how he could afford to tithe until his bills were paid. *But the tithe was not his to use for bills.* Art was startled when that thought came. It was true: the tithe was a returning to God, not a gift. All of these patriarchs had tithed, and how they had prospered! Art did not want to do anything, or fail to do anything that could delay his prosperity. From his next paycheck he took the ten percent out first, for God, and blessed it. Payments to creditors that month were smaller, but the next month good things started happening.

The next-door neighbor decided to take her old job back, and asked Jean to take care of her three children. Money for this took care of groceries and most of the utilities. Payments to creditors increased; Art became almost excited each payday as the end of his indebtedness seemed nearer and nearer. He continued to use affirmations that had helped him, after the healing had come and his finances were well and strong.

"There is no lack in my life. I have plenty of money to pay for everything we need. I bless my creditors and they quickly receive all their money. There is order in my financial affairs now. I am financially sound and well now. I get a large paycheck. I am getting prosperous rapidly. I am wealthy now. I remember where my money and all my good comes from: it all comes from God. I tithe my money to God as my financial 'thank you' for all He does for me. I am rich in ideas and money, as well as in health and happiness."

The first time he used these statements he felt he was not telling the truth, but he knew that these things were all true about the spiritual man he really was. He kept working with his thinking, and rich results came. At the end of the year he got an unlooked-for bonus from his company; a man who had owed his father money, years before, paid Art. His finances were wonderfully healed.

Another man searched his attitude toward money and listened to what he was saying, because he wanted to get past the place where he was constantly having to demonstrate money for emergencies. He thought he knew the truth about substance and its availability, but something was wrong. Something in his thinking needed to be changed, healed. He discovered that that something was fear. He was surprised. He became aware that there was a feeling in his hands when he wrote checks, a little constricting fear inside him when he spent money. Perhaps subconsciously he felt that the check he was writing was going to deplete his resources; maybe he had a guilt feeling about buying; maybe he was thinking inside that he couldn't afford the purchase, or shouldn't have it. He realized that it was fear he needed to heal, not the financial state of his affairs. No healing of any kind can come about as long as there is fear. Fear closes off channels, whether they are blood channels or money channels.

Before this man purchased anything he tried to remember to say: "*I am not afraid of spending this. I have plenty of money. I do not have to be afraid. God gives me wisdom and good judgment so I do not buy unwisely. I buy what I should. I trust Him. I do not need to be afraid. I have plenty, plenty, plenty!*"

His fear left. His emergencies seemed to cease. He found that he had plenty for all his needs as new avenues of income opened up for him. His financial condition was permanently healed.

We do not need to have a "sick" income or a "sick" bank account. We do not have to be fearful about money. We can remember where our money comes from, what it really is. We can keep ourself alert in our thinking and feeling about money and income. We need never despair over our financial situation. We know it can be healed with God's help and direction.

I praise and bless my money today. It comes from God, my Father. It provides all my needs. If I need more, my Father provides the channels for the increase to come. I am not afraid of lack, for I know the Father has unlimited substance that can be formed to meet all my needs. I am open to His ideas and I follow them; I have plenty, plenty, plenty! My finances are completely healed now.

XI
Healing Others

Whenever we're around sick people we like to make them comfortable, do things for them. Most of all, we wish we could make them well. After we have experienced the wonder of a spiritual healing, we want others to have the same thing happen to them. We want everyone to know that he does not have to stay sick, that he can be healed. But we feel inadequate. Even if we have been the channel through which our own healing came, we don't feel qualified to do the same thing for anyone else. We don't feel good enough or spiritual enough.

Not only did Ann learn that she could be a channel for healing for another person, she learned principles that can help in all healing work, principles that have been a long time used by metaphysicians. Ann had been reading, studying, and thinking about spiritual healing during the lake vacation she and her two daughters were enjoying. One day started as usual with a swim and breakfast. Then the girls went down to the beach to play, and Ann went to her study. Less than five minutes later, everything changed.

"Mama, Mama," Annette, the younger girl, screamed, "Jane's fallen and she's hurt!" She was out of breath as she ran into the cottage, her face dirty and tearstained. "Hurry!"

Ann hurried. Jane was a crumpled mass of sand, dirt, and blood. Ann closed her eyes, to stay with the first rule she had learned: *Refuse to be disturbed by any appearance of disease or hurt.* She knew she could not help Jane if she let herself be upset. She prayed for calm as she remembered a second rule: *Do not be upset or disturbed. Look to the Father and look only to Him. Know that healing is already started so you do not need to be anxious. Stay aware of God's presence. Do not judge by appearances. Look to the healing, not to the hurt or the sickness.*

This was not easy to do with all the dirt and blood, with Jane's crying. Ann made herself talk calmly to both girls. She said to them what she had been repeating to herself: "We know the healing is taking place now. We know God is with us. We know God is taking care of you, Jane. He's showing me what to do to help you feel better. No matter how you hurt and look, Jane, you're all right. You are God's child and He is taking perfect care of you now. You are being healed perfectly right now."

It was difficult to keep her mind on the healing and not wonder how deep the cuts were. It took much calmness on her part to calm the girls and their fears. Carefully she felt over Jane's body. Then she helped her stand, even though she cried, "It hurts, it hurts!" Slowly they made their way up to the cabin. Ann gently cleaned away the sand and the blood, trying not to look at the deep scrapes and bruises. She kept talking to Jane, reminding her that she was God's child and that His love for her would and could heal every hurt place. She reminded Jane of her own healings. When Ann had done all she could to make the child comfortable, she read to her. Exhausted physically and emotionally, the little girl soon slept. Then Ann held Annette for a few minutes and they both went to sleep in a large rockingchair.

They were awakened by Jane's screams: "I can't see, I can't see!" Again, Ann had to close her eyes and not look at the physical evidence. She dared not lose sight of the perfect Jane, free from hurt and blemish. Ann was more sure of herself now than she had been before. She was able to say calmly: "Jane, stop screaming. You *can* see. You're not helping the healing at all by crying and threshing around. You must be still. Don't be afraid. Remember who you are and Who is your helper and healer."

Her words helped quiet her own fears. She knew that anxiety dissipates energy and she needed all the physical and emotional energy possible. Carefully she wiped the accumulated matter from her daughter's eyes, thinking only of the clear brown eyes behind the puffed flesh. Ann thrilled as she recognized that she actually was not seeing the condition of her daughter but her perfect self. She knew without any doubt that healing was taking place. She, the healer, was healed of all belief in the condition. She had read time and again that this was what had to happen: *before the healer can be a channel for healing, he must be healed.*

Jane slept that night. The next morning she was better, interested only in seeing "how awful I look." Then she was up wanting breakfast. All traces of the accident were gone in a few days. They had all learned the basic rules of healing: not to be afraid, not to judge by appearances, to look to the healing rather than the condition, to know God can and will heal, and to expect the healing.

We can also help when people who need healings are not with us. Many of us have experienced healings through the prayers of Silent Unity. Many of us have had healings through prayers of friends, relatives, ministers, counselors. Often we can accept this but we don't think we can do the same thing for other people. When we understand God's omnipresence and His operation in timelessness and spacelessness, we can comprehend that out thoughts too are both timeless and spaceless, and that it is as easy for us to pray for a person thousands of miles away as it is for us to do spiritual work for a person in the same room with us. Most of us are as Beth was when she was asked by a friend to pray for the woman's brother.

Beth was startled and hesitant. The woman mistook her hesitancy for belief that the brother could not be healed spiritually. Beth hurried to reassure her. "Of course, he can be," Beth said quickly. This was one thing she was sure about. She had known many spiritual healings, many that had come through prayers of people for others. She knew that, for her friend's sake, she had to try. She didn't feel she knew enough, but she would use what she did know.

The wonderful thing is that we never need to wait to help others with healing until we know all about it. We simply have to use what we know at the time. When we use what we know, greater, deeper understanding always comes. We add to our comprehension of Truth every time we use any of it. Conversely, if we don't use what we understand and know with faith, we are likely to lose what we have. All Beth told her friend was that she would pray.

Never had she felt so humble and inadequate. At the same time, she believed that this was an opportunity for her to find out if she did have prayer power and could contact the Source of all good for others. Nothing would ever make her happier, she knew, than to be able to help people through prayer.

Her prayer was simple and fervent and she said it out loud: "Father, I know that You are all power. I know You are all the power there is. I know Your power can heal this man. I pray that he is now open and receptive to receive Your healing power. I know too that he can be healed now, perfectly and without delay. I know it doesn't matter what doctors or anyone else have said about his condition, because I know the Truth about him and about everyone. We are all made in Your image and likeness and, as we know this, our bodies respond and become whole and perfect. I pray that this man can know this Truth now and be healed."

She sat perfectly still for several minutes. An inner stillness came, and she was calmer than she had ever been before. She lost all concern over whether or not she could be the channel of healing for her friend's brother. She was at peace and she knew she didn't have to pray any more. Her friend called late that night to tell her the good news: her brother was out of danger. "You did it," she told Beth.

Beth quickly denied this. "No, no, not I. It is always the Father. All any of us can do is open the way for Him to heal. It would be such a responsibility if *we* had to do the healing."

It would be an awesome responsibility even if we had to turn on or make the law work. All that we have to do, fortunately, is know that the law works, and expect it to work. We cannot make God work His healing power; we need only to know that He *does* heal. Knowing that the Father does the healing, we go to Him and not to the person. This can be confusing until we think about Jesus Christ at the tomb of his friend Lazarus. He paid no attention at all to Lazarus or the tomb. He didn't even call Lazarus' name at first. He didn't indicate that He was thinking most about His friend. Instead, He called out to God. His healing conversation was with God, not with the man buried in the tomb. So it must be with our healing prayers.

We may use the sick person's name in our prayers but we are not really paying attention to him; we certainly aren't paying any mind at all to his condition. We aren't trying to change him or get him to do anything or even think anything. We are simply calling on the healing law of life and wholeness to do its perfect work in him and for him.

Even when we are in a position where we cannot help being consciously aware of physical conditions, we can keep our prayer mind on God and not on the physical. The illness, the physical dis-ease are the appearances. The real man, the God man, the spiritual man is always all right. As we turn from appearances to this real man we call the God nature, the God power, forth to heal and perfect. Each time our mind comes back to the physical appearances, we deliberately turn it toward God and healing. As we do this, we enter the presence of God. We come to the place where we are both reaching out to God and reaching in to Him. This is our God, the God we are—the God within and the God in all things outside us, in all people and in all circumstances, the one Power and the one Presence.

In this Presence we feel an at-one-ment with God that is different from any other time. It is in this Presence that we contact the healing power that heals the person for whom we are praying. This is our part and it is all we have to do: become one with the Father, knowing that His power is ours to use, that since He is all health, then we or anyone for whom we pray can share this health.

Sometimes this feeling of oneness is a feeling of deep love. Lucy experienced this. A young cousin had been very ill. He was not responding to treatment and the family was given no hope for his recovery. Lucy knew they had all been praying; she had, too. As she sat in the hallway outside his hospital room, she thought about how she was praying. She was a little aghast that she was praying a pleading prayer, a "Please, God" prayer. She had not realized that she had slipped back into the old anthropomorphic idea of God as a big man to be placated and begged for favors. What an injustice to the God she really had, a God not bound by any kind of physical characteristics, Who did not have to be begged or bargained with for favors but Who wanted to give all good to His children! How glad she was that she had this kind of God!

Lucy was warmed, she was filled with a wonderful glow. She felt alive as she never had felt before. Then she thought of her cousin.

She was no longer afraid for him. She no longer thought there was any possibility of his not getting well. Filled with love, she had no room for anxiety. Her cousin was part of God's love too. All was well with him. She did not have to be fearfully concerned. She felt this wonderful love all around her cousin and in him, as it was with her and in her.

She was not surprised when the family was told later that evening that the boy's fever had gone down and that he was sleeping. Pulse, pressure, all body functions were normal. Lucy felt love flooding over her again as she thanked God for her cousin's perfect healing.

It is never work when we pray for healing for others. It is effortless, easy, happy, joyous. It doesn't have to take much time. One man found it took only a second; another that it took only three words.

Sometimes it is good to have things happen unexpectedly. Our reactions can tell us a lot about ourself. Sometimes we are wiser and stronger than we think. Seth found that he was reacting in a healing way when a secretary in his office collapsed one afternoon. There was instant commotion and alarm in the office. Someone said that she had these blackouts every now and then and that they were serious. She always had to be in bed for several days afterwards. Someone called an ambulance. Seth heard himself saying almost before he thought the words: "She's going to be all right. She'll be all right before the ambulance gets here."

He was surprised that he was not upset, as the others were. He knew that he believed in spiritual healing and the possibility of instantaneous healing, although he had never experienced it himself. He knew too that this girl was God's child, that she was one with God. He didn't really pray in words; he was simply very quiet. It was from the depths of this calmness that he saw the girl regaining consciousness, saw the color coming back in her face, saw her getting up, heard her saying she was all right. In a very short time she was back at her desk. The ambulance call was canceled.

Seth had not been disturbed by appearances; he had not accepted as true about the girl what others said. He knew healing was possible, and he expected it to happen without delay.

Joel's three healing words were, "This is passing." A business associate had what appeared to be a mild stroke. The man fell as he was about to enter the office elevator. The left side of his body was partially paralyzed. Joel was the first to reach him. As he leaned over the man, he said, "Bob, this is passing." He thought the man heard him. Joel remained very calm. Then there was a change inside him, a little like the wind changing. There was a warm, happy feeling, a good feeling inside him. Joel had a sense of joy and he thought: "Father, thank You. It has passed." Whatever it was, it *had* passed. The man's left side, his arm and his leg straightened. He was helped up and he was all right.

We all learn from such experiences. We learn that we must be calm, we must be still inside even if we are doing things that need to be done. We learn to turn at once to the healing and away from the condition. From this stillness within will come the right word for us to say or the right thing to do. From this stillness will come healing love, energy, life. We never have to become healers, in any special sense of the meaning of the word. We only become *knowers* of the Truth of being. We see or know of the body discord, but we do not pay any attention to it. Our attention is on God all the time.

It is good to think how everywhere Jesus went, healings took place. It is good to think about Peter, who became so aware of his oneness with the Father that even his shadow healed. It was never what the disciples did that healed, because they rarely did anything. It was their oneness with the Father. It was what they knew about themselves and about the people they healed. So we keep experiencing the oneness, we continue to be undisturbed by physical appearances, we never falter in our faith and sureness that healing is possible and has started. We expect the healing to come regardless of what others think or say. We rest content in the knowledge that we can be channels for healing. We know the healing law and we expect it to work for us. With each healing we help bring about comes greater knowledge and confidence, not in ourself but in God's available healing power. This is how we heal others—not we ourself, but the Father.

XII
Healing Can Be Permanent

Sometimes we are so sick that even to be a little better would be a miracle; sometimes we would settle for a night of ease from pain. Usually we want a complete and permanent healing, and we should have it. We can. This is our good news, the good story for us, our own special gospel. Not only can we be healed, but we can stay that way. We do not have to have chronic ill health; we don't have to be uncomfortable in August, sick in January, or in March. We don't have to have repetitions of the same physical discomfort. Too many people have had permanent spiritual healings for it not to be possible for us to have them too. But there are several things we have to be certain about.

We have to be sure that we don't want in any way to be sick, that we don't in the least enjoy the attention we get when we are not well. We have to check to see if we are claiming our sickness as "my hay fever," "my weak back," "my nervous stomach." *I do not want to be sick, no, I don't! I do not claim any body disharmony. I claim only health and healthful conditions for my body.*

We have to be sure that we understand that our body is the temple of the living God and that, as such, it must be whole, sound, perfect, alive with health and beautiful in operation. We cannot enjoy perfect, lasting health until we do know this, and take care of our body. *My body is the temple of the living God. I treat my body with respect and love.*

We do the practical physical things to take care of

our body. We keep it clean inside and out, we get enough exercise, the right foods and liquids, enough sleep, relaxation.

We are careful about our thoughts, our emotions, our words. We think health, we speak health, we react emotionally in a healthful way. We are alert to all our emotional reactions. We are careful not to hold any grudges, resentments, hurts, hates. We know that these negative emotions can make us sick, keep us sick even years after we have expressed them.

We keep our conscious and subconscious mind packed with healthful ideas. We don't think sick and we don't speak sick. Even if everyone in the room is talking sickness, we don't join in. We silently bless everyone and know that anyone anywhere can be healed. We think of the woman who touched the hem of Jesus Christ's garment and was healed; we remember Peter's healing handkerchief. We can pray that there is so much healing faith in our thought and feeling that it can be tapped by anyone seeking a spiritual healing. *I think only healthful thoughts, I speak only words of health.*

In effecting a healing, we often have to stand firm for a long time. We know that when we do stand firm we are following Jesus Christ's injunction to "only believe." When we stand firm we are not being double-minded and we are not as "one that wavers." *I am never discouraged about my healing. I stand firm. I expect to be healed. I never change my mind. I am steadfast in expecting my healing.*

As we stand firm, we come to the place where we can completely trust God and wait on Him to do the healing we desire. *I trust and believe in God's healing power. I expect His power to work in this situation.*

It is when we get to this place of expectancy, particularly instant expectancy, that we are ready for healings that are permanent. In a permanent healing, there is no room for any doubt or wishful thinking. When the healing comes, there must not be even a tiny bit of feeling that it won't last. There must be no sense of "this is too good to be true" or "this can't last." We have to know all through us, in every corner of our conscious and subconscious mind, that no healing is too much for us to expect and to have, that no healing is too marvelous to last.

When we get to the place where our thoughts have permanent healing in them, with no trace of the possibility of sickness, then we can expect permanent healing. Genie did.

Genie didn't have any problem about faith. She was born with faith and so, when she understood the possibilities of spiritual healing, she had a lot of faith power to add to her new understanding. She used the combination of faith with understanding and had several minor healings of cuts, burns, and colds. Temporary things, little things, she called them. Then her faith and her understanding faced a big test. A growth was discovered during a physical checkup. It increased and there were some symptoms that were alarming. Genie was scared. She had a husband and three small children.

"Then it came to me," she said, "I had forgotten all about God. They say people often pray only when they get in a tight spot. But I got in a situation and forgot that God was always there to help. God had certainly helped me and healed me before. Somehow I had tried to meet this emergency all by myself. I apologized to Him." She smiled. "Yes, I apologized for waiting so long to ask Him for healing, for not remembering that it didn't matter what the need was, He could take care of it.

"I thought again about how Jesus Christ healed 'all manner of sickness.' Then I remembered all the healings we had had as a family and all the spiritual healings I had ever known about.

"Two things came to me. The first was that the only way I can grow actually is spiritually, and any other kind of growth is not real. Then I remembered the words, 'The word of God is living and active, sharper than any two-edged sword, . . . and discerning the thoughts and intentions of the heart.' The last of the verse made me think of spiritual surgery. That was the kind of surgery I wanted."

She made two strong affirmations and used them over and over, all that day and most of the night: *"There is no growth but spiritual growth, and I grow spiritually. There are no false growths in my body."* She wanted to grow spiritually! O, she wanted more than a physical healing. She wanted to come through this experience a much better person, a more knowing person, a more faith-filled person. Her other affirmation was based on the verse in Hebrews:

"God is my surgeon. I need no other. His love is doing whatever needs to be done now and I am completely, perfectly, and permanently healed now."

Within less than two months Genie was healed. The growth passed from her body easily. There was no need for convalescence and there has been no recurrence.

Sometimes it is amusing what makes us get busy to bring about a spiritual healing. It was a girl who made Fred give more than lip service to a belief in the healing power of the Father. Fred was allergic to roses. Serums, shots, pills helped some but the best thing was to "stay away from them." Then he met the first girl he really liked from the moment he saw her. Fred had never been so "turned on" about any girl before; he was twenty-seven years old and ready. She was so unusual that he assumed she did something out of the ordinary. She did: she grew roses commercially, supplying several florists! She loved roses and experimented with new types!

There was moonlight the night of their first date. Everything was soft and beautiful. The night and the moon and the girl made Fred decide that his rose allergy had to go. He refused to be in bondage any longer. He decided to rely on God as the only power in his life. He was going to give nothing but God power over him.

"I refuse to be in bondage to anything except God. I am free from any false bondage. I set myself free. Roses are beautiful and I enjoy them. I like roses and they like me. God created me and He created roses. We can get along together in peace and harmony."

His freedom came. He did not marry the girl (for reasons that had nothing to do with roses). However, he still thinks she was one of the most wonderful happenings in his whole life. If she hadn't come along he might not have been healed. The love affair wasn't permanent, but the healing has been.

When we are healed, we want everyone to be healed. One way we can help spread healing power is to pray with understanding for people we read about in the newspapers or hear about over radio or television. This is one way we can share what we have been given. Here too we turn from the horror or the hurt to the healing. We think of wholeness and perfect healing, and not of the "facts" of the situation as we hear or read them. We can be so at one that the Father's healing power is turned on for whomsoever is open and receptive to healing.

We will probably never know the outcome of these healing prayers. We don't need to. Our only need is to send them. One woman was very faithful in praying for all she heard about who were in need of healing. Many times reports on conditions changed very quickly. It did not matter what brought about the change; the healing came. There is so much need for healing in the world today that we can give unlimited healing service to mankind with our healing prayers. In this, as in any healing prayers, we know that we are never the healers. We are only the knowers of the Truth.

Our role is to rise above the situation and not be held down by appearances. A woman who was vitally interested in learning more about spiritual healing had a most revealing dream one night. There were many people in need of healing in a room and in the dream she was floating about them; she was completely separate but somehow she was with their healing. In her dream she was aware that the healing was going on as it was needed but it was not part of her. We too must rise above the health needs. We do not watch the conditions and we do not watch for indications that healing is being accomplished. Neither are we impatient or in a hurry for the healing. We keep our mind stayed on God. We turn to God at the first moment of working for healing and we keep our mind and all our attention on Him until the healing comes. We do not have to be concerned with the working of the healing power; all we have to know is that there is this healing power and that it works. We do not even need to be concerned about whether the healing is going to be permanent or complete. We are concerned only with our expectancy, our understanding, our faith, our trust.

We know spiritual healings are possible. We know many things we can do to help keep our body healthy. We know how to feed our conscious and subconscious mind with health thoughts. We keep our emotions healthy. We heal our memories and our failures. We expect health and we expect healings, not only for ourself but for others, people we know and people we don't know, people who live near us and people who live around the world from us.

We decree health for ourself and for all mankind. We know healing is possible for all. As we become more proficient in living a health-filled life and in letting the healing power work in our life, we are more effective for others. We expect health and we expect permanent healings. We develop permanent health attitudes and expectations. Eventually we get to the place where we no longer hope for a healing, to the place where we can accept a healing the instant we sense a need for it.

I expect healing.

I expect healing now.

I expect my healing to be permanent.

I accept my healing. It is here now.

Thank God, I am healed, permanently healed now!

Helps to Spiritual Healing

The second half of this book contains specific helps for healing body and mental dis-ease by spiritual methods. Suggestions are given as to metaphysical causes, and for changes in ways of thinking and feeling. These have all been used successfully by people who needed these particular healings. Of course this is not a comprehensive encyclopedia of physical problems. However, the reader can adapt any of the healing suggestions given to his particular need. Fundamentally, the healing methods are similar: certain attitudes, beliefs, habits, actions need to be changed to give the God-given natural healing ability of the body a chance to function, and certain prayers, denials with affirmations, new ways of thinking, feeling, and speaking can help the healing come.

What others have found effective in getting their spiritual healings, anyone can do. Knowing that others have effected healings helps us become more objective about our own condition and, of course, it makes us more hopeful and confident of bringing about our own healing.

We learn that despite the length of time we have been suffering, the situation can change. Charles Fillmore said that it is the divine idea of perfection that restores the body. It does not matter how long it takes for us to get this idea of perfection. The important thing is to get it! Our body is always trying to be perfect: it starts instantly to heal when anything happens to it. Doctors work with this inner power;

they do everything they can to make it easy for the body to get about its healing business. Charles Fillmore also says that we can feel a flow of health instantly when we hold the right thoughts—healing thoughts about our body—and that healings often come simply by closing the mind to the condition and holding to Divine Mind. We hold to the idea of perfection and the truth that our body is a temple of the living God (which is only another way of saying that our body is spiritual), and we know that the perfect mold or pattern for our body is waiting for our words and feelings to re-create it, strengthen it, heal, revitalize, re-energize, and restore it.

Thoughts, feelings, and words are the healing instruments we use. Becoming one with the Father lets the God power within us work. Jesus Christ, of course, was the one man who achieved perfect oneness. However, He promised that we too could achieve all that He did, and more. What He had, what He did, we have the potentiality to have and to do. As He was able to heal, so are we.

This oneness is not interfered with if we have others helping us. It can be there no matter how many doctors, surgeons, psychiatrists, or nurses may be working to help us. The oneness includes them too for they are also channels through which one Mind, Divine Mind, can operate to bring about our healing. We know that we never do the healing, that God is the healer. He is in charge of our body as well as all of our life and affairs, He works through us and through anyone concerned with us. His Mind is in control—guiding, directing, inspiring the help given us. And whatever is being done, regardless of how we are trying for health, it is all for healing and not for sickness. This is the way we get a health consciousness.

Our consciousness is made up of all that we are aware of, and we want to start quickly to be aware of health and healing and unaware of the dis-ease. We must let go of all ideas of sickness, weakness, pain and insist that our mind, body, and emotions are attuned to healing. We loose our fears, we increase our knowing and understanding of ourself and our ability to heal; we encourage our faith to stay strong while the healing comes.

We learn that *this* moment is the only moment we need to be concerned about. We do not have to waste a single moment regretting anything we may or may not have done, said, felt, believed in the past. *What we think now, what we feel now, what we say now, is all that matters.* We do not have to be concerned about this afternoon, tonight, tomorrow morning, next week, next year, or any time. Now is the time we start our healing. Now is the time we know for sure that our body wants healing, that it is equipped to heal itself, that it is ready for healing.

It is so easy for us to get used to the idea of sickness. It is humanly easy to be discouraged about our physical condition. It is sometimes difficult to expect healing, but we can. Where there has been dis-ease, there can be ease; where there has been weakness, there can be strength; where there has been tension and pain, there can be freedom. Where there was fear because of physical appearances, there can be confidence of recovery. We get to the place where we stop wasting time; we reach out our thoughts immediately when there is a need, we stretch them out to health, and we get well. We understand why Jesus asked the man, "Do you want to be healed? . . . And at once the man was healed." We begin to say "yes" quickly to spiritual healing.

We become alert to our moods, our emotions, what we are saying and thinking that could have an adverse effect on our body. We change whatever needs to be changed. We do not delay. We do not wait.

We can control our part in the healing. We start with what we know now. We don't need to know everything there is to know about spiritual healing. We choose health today: it is almost that simple. We want health, so we think about health. We stop thinking about the need for healing. We think only of the healing, and the healing power within us. The more we use this healing power, what we know about healing, the easier it becomes.

In each case when someone used the affirmations and denials, the prayers suggested in this part of this book, he reached out for the consciousness of allness and oneness, he became aware of the one Power and one Presence in his body. Healings came for little and big needs, and for needs of all types.

We learn. We stop looking at the sick condition and look instead to the Father within. We keep our mind stayed on God, paying no attention to our sick body. If we keep alert to God, we won't have time to watch our body and it can go about its job of healing. We do not have to be concerned about how the body heals. We do not need medical or scientific understanding, only spiritual. We simply give the body a chance to heal. We keep our mind on God, and the healing comes.

Accidents

Some of us have so many accidents that we feel we must have been singled out by Fate to have more than anybody else. Some of us say that we are accident-prone. We think we are so awkward, so clumsy, that we never do things right and things happen to us. Most of us think a lot about accidents other people have, about accidents we almost had, about accidents we may have.

When we have an accident consciousness we are giving accidents power in our life. We are thinking in a double-minded way; we are actually putting something ahead of God. We are, in fact, believing that there are places we can be where God is not, that there are times when we are away from His protecting Presence. We know that such separation is impossible, for God is never away from us, closer than hands or feet, closer even than breathing. When we remember this we have a feeling of safety that nothing else can give. If God is always with us, there can be nothing to fear. This is the way we lose the belief in the inevitability of accidents, of uncertainty about the future. We become secure, protected, guided to do the right thing when we are handling dangerous tools, when we drive, when we fly, when we walk.

We stop expecting accidents to happen; we start expecting good and only good to happen to us. We can start expecting the same good for others too.

I expect only good to happen today. I attract only good today. I go with God today. Wherever I am, He is. I work with Him. I travel with Him. He is with me always, protecting me, guiding me, leading me in safe places, in safe ways. There is nothing to fear. I go with God everywhere.

(We can say the same things for others by using "you" instead of "I.")

A long time ago it was customary to say, "Go with God," in farewell. The blessing is still used in some parts of the world today. It is good for us to get in the habit of blessing others with this good-bye either silently or aloud.

We think safety, not accidents. We take intelligent precautions, we observe safety laws, we keep our equipment in good mechanical condition. We keep ourself rested and well. We work and travel without fear or expectation of harm.

God is with me wherever I am, whatever I am doing. I think safety, I act safely, I am safe.

We spend more mental and emotional time expecting good. We know God's protecting love goes before us always, making our way safe. We know that the white light of the Christ can surround us, keeping out all harm and also protecting us from doing things that we should not.

The love of God goes before me now directing and guiding, protecting me. The white light of the Christ surrounds me at all times and I am safe. I behave in a safe manner. I help others act safely. I am constantly aware of God's protecting Presence with me.

When we know that we do not need to be afraid of accidents, our life is much happier. One man overcame his fear of accidents by using this prayer affirmation each time he got into his car: "*I am in tune with infinity.*"

He believed that if he could keep in tune with infinity, he would never be anywhere he shouldn't be.

But what about injuries through accidents?

First, we know that nothing has happened to God's man, our perfect self; the mold and pattern of our perfection is intact no matter what appears to be the condition of the physical body. We at once thank God for His life which is always part of us and for His healing power which is already at work. We know too that every person who is helping us in any way is being guided by Divine Mind to do the right things for us. We know that everything is in divine order, that God is in control.

We keep our mind on perfect healing; we determinedly and resolutely turn our eyes from the physical appearance to the healing. We do not take time to wonder why the accident happened, what we or anyone else may have done that was wrong, either before or at the time of the accident.

The important and immediate thing is to see that we are not doing anything to interfere with the body's healing processes by being emotional, despairing, fearful, or condemnatory either of ourself or of the person who seems to be responsible for what happened. Later we can decide what was wrong in our thinking or actions; were we in too much of a hurry, were we angry, were we emotionally disturbed, tired, taking a chance? Whatever our answers to these and similar questions, we do not condemn ourself. We learn what we need to from the experience, resolve not to let it happen again, and redouble our efforts to eliminate any remnants of an accident consciousness we have.

Healing is taking place in my body now. There is no delay. I do not interfere with this healing by being fearful, resentful, complaining, emotional. I keep myself relaxed so that the currents of healing life can flow through my body making me sound. The miracle of healing is taking place in my body now. I expect healing and it comes. I have a wonderful body. It heals no matter what is to be healed.

God heals me. He "binds up the crippled, and strengthens the weak." I know God heals. He is healing me now. I rest quietly, knowing the healing is taking place right now. I am healed perfectly, wonderfully, miraculously now. Thank God!

Alcoholics

Statistics show that every year there are more heavy drinkers who harm themselves in many ways—physically, psychologically, economically, and socially—by their drinking. Among these are chronic alcoholics, problem drinkers, compulsive drinkers. Continued excessive drinking deteriorates body and mind and cuts down life expectancy. While these heavy drinkers seem to be able to stand a great deal of self-abuse, they never function at anywhere near their possible capacity, and the harm they do others is often as great as what they do to themselves.

Families are ruined, business careers and talents dissipated. But healing can come.

We go back to causes. Sometimes drinking begins as an attempt to escape unpleasantness, difficulty. Sometimes the individual has been angry with life, hasn't received the treatment he felt he should have, hasn't been the success he wanted to be, feels that he is alone against the world. Whether he realizes it or not he is feeling separation from God and from good. He is not sure of God's love for him. As his problem becomes more serious, he cannot think of God in any way other than as a condemning God, for he is condemning himself. He is caught in a real dilemma: caught between wanting to get away from himself, all that he is and all that he isn't, and hating what he is becoming. To escape this he drinks more, and the unhappy circle goes around and around until he stops long enough to want to quit drinking, long enough to realize that God's love is waiting and ready to help him.

During this period noncondemning, loving prayers can help. Those around him can help by never thinking of the person as an alcoholic but as a perfect child of God, affirming that he is accepting inner guidance whether he knows where it comes from or not. These statements proved effective for the wife of one alcoholic:

"*You are the perfect child of God. God loves you. God always has loved you; He always will love you. You lose all desire to drink to excess. You become your true self now. God is helping you in every way.*"

A man who, as he said, came to himself long enough to find God was waiting for him, found sufficient help to stay with his resolve not to drink by using these affirmations:

"God is with me every instant helping me respect my body and my mind. He tells me what to do and I am too busy to waste any more time drinking. God does not condemn me; neither do I condemn myself. God has set me free to be the person I am meant to be. There is no desire for drink in me any more. Thank God!"

It has been believed that those who drink are really searching for something they don't have, for happiness, inspiration. Erroneously the drinker expects alcohol to stimulate him; instead it depresses. The first effects of the depressant can be relaxing, bringing a temporary relief from unpleasantness. Then comes the lowering of mental and physical awareness, and lack of control of body and emotions.

For the searcher meditation can be a help, but it must be a purposeful meditation. Simply to quiet the mind is not the answer. It is essential to take a word, a thought, a God quality into the stillness as a protective focus for the mind. The word might be peace, love, strength, joy, release, wisdom, courage, abundance. Those who have sought inspiration from alcohol often find great creative stimulation through meditation. With this source of inspiration, desire for drink left one man. He had doubted that anything could be different after only being still for a few minutes. He found that there was a big change. He won a contest with an idea that came to him in meditation; he had so many ideas for his job that he didn't have time to drink! He used these affirmations:

"God is my strength, my guide, my protector, my inspiration. I need no false helps. My life is being changed for the better. I no longer want to drink. I am a new person. I am completely changed. My life is new. My life is filled with all kinds of exciting new good. I am an exciting new person. I am the person God intended me to be. He is helping me every step of the way. He tells me what to do and I do it."

Allergies

Allergies are indications of the body's adverse reaction to certain things in the environment or something that has been taken into the body. We are always reacting. We react to people, conditions, circumstances, things. If we have physical allergies we should search for our people allergies. How are we reacting to people in our life? People are more important in this respect than circumstances, because people make a situation what it is. Sometimes we say that people get under our skin. This can be literally true. We can let our feelings about people make us break out in a rash or welts. We can let people make us physically sick. We can let them give us headaches, backaches.

Many physical allergies have disappeared when

individuals recognized that they were reacting to other people, and stopped. In each case the person saw God in other people and he could not react adversely to God—so the allergy was taken care of. Some statements used were:

"I do not react to people. I feel God in them. I know God is in them. I am in harmony with God. Therefore I am in harmony with all people, for God is in all. No person disturbs me any more. I react only with love. I no longer react physically to anyone or anything in my world."

Almost the same affirmations were used by a man who was allergic to several plants on his ranch. He needed to stay there, to be around these growing things. He knew he was the one who had to change, and he did. He refused to be allergic any longer. He refused to think that anything in God's world could harm him. He refused to react with physical symptoms of allergy.

"I react only to good, and I react only in good ways. Nothing disturbs me, no person, no circumstance, no thing. Nothing irritates my body. I am free to go and come as I need to, and nothing interferes with my health or well-being now."

Other decrees that brought relief from allergies were: *"I am free from all resentment toward people or happenings in my past and present; I am free from all hate and from all fear. I am in harmony with everything and everybody now. Nothing disturbs me mentally, physically, or emotionally. I react mentally with understanding and intelligence. I react emotionally with love. I do not react physically to anything in my life."*

Another successful declaration was: *"All irrita-*

tions are gone. I am at peace in mind, body, and emotions. I have no allergies now."

Arms, Hands, Legs, Feet

We contact the world with our arms, hands, legs, and feet. We also communicate with our eyes, our words, and our tone of voice. Sometimes our body "talks" to other people but it is mainly through our hands and arms that we invite or repel people, and with our legs and feet that we go to them or away from them.

Metaphysically we think of feet as our understanding. They make our contact with the world, while our hands are the doers of our desires and thoughts. Our feet and hands have much to do with how we feel and how well we function. When our feet hurt, we are hard to live with; when our hands hurt, it is difficult to do what we are supposed to be doing. Our hands and feet are marvels of creation, so intricately designed that no two are alike. Baby footprints, fingerprints have long been used to prove identity. Our feet are created to carry us miles and miles each day, year after year. Our hands are almost unbelievable. If our hands or feet were constructed of the hardest metal, within a year it would be worn thin, perhaps completely demolished by all the wear we give them. But our hands, with a minimum of care and consideration, show little if any wear and tear. Our feet protest the loudest when we put shoes on them that do not fit properly.

Legs and arms carry us places and carry loads. Shoulders and hips, knees and elbows and ankles all must be strong too, flexible, free-moving. We help them do their work by keeping our body free from tension. Our joints must be free-moving, our bone structure straight, our muscles strong, and all free from swellings or pain. They can be.

Faith strengthens muscles wherever they are; wisdom straightens out things including bones; love always heals. Daily we can massage our feet, legs, hands, arms and tell them: *"Faith strengthens you, love heals you, wisdom straightens you."* This was the healing statement a woman used for her feet that had become slightly mishapen from poorly fitting shoes.

Another woman used this: *I bless my feet for they are messengers for God. His love dissolves all hardness in them, erases all blemishes, deflates all swelling. My joints move freely for I am completely free from tension.*

"Any hardness in my heart is gone as God's love fills it, and this love is the perfect oil to lubricate my joints. Freedom from tension keeps everything moving as it should. Love oils and keeps my body 'hinges' free from 'squeaks' and hurts."

We see our hands as instruments for doing God's work. He has to work through us, and most of what He needs to have us do is done through our hands. So our hands are God's special agents.

My hands are God's hands. I am grateful for all

they do and I bless them. They become more beautiful each day as I consciously use them to express God's qualities in my life. I create with my hands. I express love with my hands. I heal with my hands. I give life with my hands. I keep my hands open to receive the good that is mine and I keep them open to share what I have with others.

We do not try to hide our hands if they are ugly from work or from hurt. Instead, we bless them and call them beautiful. They always respond. One woman wanted both her feet and hands to be more beautiful. She prayed this way: "*Father, thank You for my hands and feet. They are beautiful. They do not ache or swell; they are perfect. My feet carry me quickly to my good; my hands receive it. You carry my burdens so my shoulders are not weighted down. All my joints move freely, completely free from tension. I praise and thank You for the wonder of my feet and legs, my hands and arms.*"

Arthritis, Rheumatism

It is understandable that the metaphysical cause given for arthritis is faultfinding, criticism, struggle, habitual anxiety, fear, resistance. Medical science defines arthritis as inflammation of a joint. What could do a better job of inflaming than criticism, resistance, or anxiety? It is also understandable that more women than men are arthritic. In this still masculine world there are fewer possibilities for women to "do something" about bothersome matters. To ease pain and relax muscles tensed under stress of discomfort, medical science uses drugs to ease tension. From these facts we get an indication of the best way to work spiritually to heal arthritis or rheumatism.

We avoid faultfinding and criticism. We do not nag. We are not afraid. We do not expect hard conditions in our life and we don't talk about our life as being hard. We learn to relax. We bless our body and picture it perfect in form, completely relaxed in every way so that all body functions can operate perfectly, without any interference. We drink in love with every mouthful of liquid, we eat love with every bite of food, we breathe in love with every breath, we think love with every thought, we express love with every word—because we know that not only is love the great healer, it is also the antidote for everything that creates arthritic conditions.

Love is the only thing that will take faultfinding out of our makeup, that will remove fear. Love can dissolve any hard deposits in joints, can loosen up joints, can flex muscles. Through love we find freedom from pain, stiffness, swelling. To help love along we take better care of our body than we ever have before. We eat the right food, we exercise, we rest. We thank our body for every bit of improvement and we constantly expect more. We expect healing.

One man who had not recognized his tendency to speak critically and to find fault (his wife knew it!)

used the following to help him start his healing: "*My thoughts are loving. My feelings toward all people and all conditions are loving. There are no hidden hurts or resentments in me. I criticize no one and no one criticizes me. I find fault with no one. I do not have time to be critical for I am busy with love. Love eases my pain, loosens my joints, straightens all crooked places. I am free from any emotional hurts and I am free from physical distress and discomfort. I hurt no one with my tongue. I do not hurt myself with sharp remarks, sharp emotions.*

"*I am gentle, loving, kind, understanding. My body responds to all this love. I am finally relaxed in my mind, in my emotions, and all through my body. Every joint is relaxed, every muscle is relaxed. I protect my body with relaxed feelings. God's love is healing my body now.*

"*I see improvement every day. I feel better each day. I am more loving each day. I am freer from tension, pain, stiffness each day. The healing is being accomplished perfectly and without delay. Thank God!*"

Beauty, Youth

We all want to be more beautiful than our mirrors say we are. We all want to be young, young, young!

Every year millions of dollars are spent in the quest for a youthful, beautiful appearance. While we keep hoping for the perfect substance to rub on our skin and hair, we know that true beauty and youthfulness comes from within. So this is where our spiritual treatment starts.

We treat the real us, the person inside. We check first to see if we are feeling old or young, homely or beautiful. There are many things people have done that have made them not only feel younger but look younger and more beautiful. Most of them have taken care of both the inner and outer man. It can help the beauty feeling along to use cosmetics that clean, soften, and smooth the skin. It can lift the spirits to smell the fragrance of soaps, lotions, and perfumes. It is necessary that we watch what we eat and drink. But what we think and feel is still more important.

Our face mirrors our feelings and thoughts. Some of our facial lines come from our thoughts and feelings. Some add character to the face; others keep beauty away. One woman found that her face changed agreeably after some time of declaring: "*I think only good thoughts. I think only happy thoughts. I think beauty, peace, order, happiness. My face reflects my thoughts. The goodness and beauty of my feelings are reflected in my face.*"

Most of us need to stop thinking about age, our own and that of others. It is too easy to place someone in an age category, thinking that at any given age he can do only certain things. We are likely to pigeonhole people by ages. Some of us react by not wanting to mark our birthdays. But birthdays are "our days," and we should not regret them or dread them or see them as markers limiting our years. They are indicators of the gift of years we have had, of the wisdom we have learned, of the happiness we have enjoyed. Because we expect still greater good, we have the bounce and expectancy of youth. We think the same way about other people: we want them to feel young with us, to feel alive, healthy, expectant of ever increasing good. We don't want to be age conscious; we want to be youth conscious, and we want others to think and feel youth too.

Ruth Gordon, the successful actress, when asked how she maintained such good health and vitality at seventy-three, replied: "I'm kind to myself. I get enough rest. I don't overeat. I take a three-mile walk every day. I treat myself like a treasure, which I am to myself."

A man who was young and handsome had more years than most people ever suspected. For a long time he had used the following: "*In every way I am alive, alert; I do not miss a trick. I appreciate the past. I enjoy the present. I look forward to the future with joyous anticipation. I am young. I am handsome. I am energetic. I am happy. I am successful. I am healthy. I am wealthy. I am wise. I am gloriously young in mind, body, and emotions.*" And he was!

Yes, we cultivate beauty and strength and youthfulness within. We cultivate youthful ideas and feelings. We see our body as beautiful and we look eagerly to new, happy, wonderful experiences. We take sensible care of our body, we watch our thinking and feeling and so we encourage inner beauty, charm, and youthfulness. Then we see it in the outer.

Thank God, I am young in mind, body, action, and appearance. Thank God, I see beauty in people and in things. I see beauty all around me in this beautiful world God made so wonderfully. Thank God, I express beauty in word and deed. Thank God, I am young and beautiful now.

Blood

We call blood "lifegiving," and it is. Blood and its circulatory system constitute a major wonder. Its functioning is a spiritual lesson. The fresh blood circulates, feeding all parts of the body, picking up used and discarded waste. Then it returns to be purified and renewed. We can take in thoughts of life and strength, we can eliminate old sick thoughts; we can be made new. Metaphysically blood conditions are believed to be the results of fear, tensions, old resentments, worries, despair. We can understand how fears and tensions can constrict arteries and veins so that they cannot do their work properly. We can understand how worry and despair can slow down the circulation, creating bad results. Again we start eliminating cause.

I am not depressed. I am not despairing. I am expectant of good. I am joyous. I am happy. My blood circulates at the rate it should; it circulates freely. It is pure, happy, living blood. God's life keeps it perfect.

If our blood pressure doesn't register as normal, we may be frightened, whether it is too low or too high. One man was quite disturbed about his high reading. High blood pressure "ran in his family." The affirmations that helped him get his blood pressure down to normal included these:

"I am free from tension and strain. I inherit only good. I am not afraid of anything for my Father is with me always. My blood pressure is normal. There is no interference with the free circulation of blood in my body. I appreciate the wondrous workings of the blood in my body rejuvenating me, healing me."

Healing from a diseased condition of the blood came when these statements were used: *"I do not have sick blood. Everything that should be in my blood is there now; anything that should not be there is eliminated at once. God is purifying my blood, renewing it, restoring it to health and perfection now."*

Another person used: *"I bless my blood and my body. I feel God's life coursing through my arteries and my veins. Every little capillary is healthy and doing its perfect work—feeding, renewing, revitalizing my body. I breathe in life and vitality and my blood is cleansed, purified, made vital again. I bless my heart for its regular, dependable pumping of my blood. I bless my lungs for their steady, dependable purifying work. All is well with my blood and with my life transportation system. My blood is healthy, alive. I am alive with the life of God. Everything in my body is healthy and whole."*

Bruises, Scars

Oh, how we don't want to have bruises and scars! Sometimes it seems that this last part of a healing is the part we don't do much about. The cut is closed and healed, the scrapes and skinned places are taken care of, but we don't work on the scars and the bruises. There are several possible reasons for this.

Maybe we think it's only a matter of time. Maybe we think they won't go away no matter what we do. Maybe we don't think they can be healed.

We have heard it said after a serious injury, "This is a scar that will not go away." We tend to accept what we're told, but we should deny it quickly. We should say, at least to ourself: "My body is constantly renewing itself. This part of it can be whole and perfect, too. It too will heal. My skin will be unblemished yet."

It helps if we remember that our spiritual body is always perfect, always intact. We have learned that if we keep our thoughts harmonious and health-filled, and if we don't allow negative ideas any room in our consciousness, the physical body will become like the spiritual one. Again we turn from the condition to the healing: we think of smooth, perfect skin, not of the scar.

If we are bruised we know that our body is equipped to take care of any mishap quickly. Tissue cells get to work at once to get the displaced blood where it belongs. Healing starts, and does not stop until all is well.

A helpful prayer of affirmation is: "*I am not*

bruised inside or out. I am not tense and I have no ill feelings, so I do not interfere with the healing that is already going on. I bless this hurt place. I know God's healing power is at work now. The bruise disappears now. God's life is active in every cell, making my body healthy and my skin smooth and perfect.

"This scar [or bruise] is not permanent. It passes quickly. No sign of the injury remains now. Thank God!"

Colds, Viruses

Until we start to take good care of our body, because we know that it is a holy temple, we are likely to be susceptible to the common cold and to viruses. Doctors tell us that the germs of both are around all the time, and we usually have to be run down and not up to par when we "get" one or the other. Yes, until we respect the physical body and guard against dis-ease thoughts we are likely to be vulnerable to attacks of cold or virus.

Metaphysically, colds indicate confusion, agitation, disturbance, a feeling of loss or shock, resentment, emotional disturbance. It's easy to see why people are susceptible. There is much confusion around; there are all kinds of shocks, losses, disturbances around all of us. We are so often in the middle of both confusion and disturbance. We don't take very good care of our body; we don't get enough rest, enough fresh air, enough exercise, the right foods. So we set ourself up for colds and viruses.

We have to be very careful about viruses. They are so very, very small. We have to guard against the tiniest negation in our thinking and speaking, for it will take only the smallest opening for a little virus microbe to enter. We don't dare let the smallest wrong thought enter our consciousness. We don't dare react the least bit negatively to anything. We don't dare let ourself be perturbed over anything. Above all, we try to be good to ourself and establish and maintain order in every part of our life.

If we get a cold, or a virus sneaks in, we start (perhaps a little belatedly) to take care of ourself. We start treating our body with respect. We go to bed and catch up on our rest. We remain calm and serene.

Some affirmations that have helped are:

"I am not perturbed by anything or anyone. No situation bothers me at all. I am serene. I am calm. I am sure that all is going to be well in my world now. There is no confusion in my thinking or in my life. My body is at work now getting rid of this cold [virus]. All I have to do is relax, rest, take care of me. I know that all is well now.

"My body is the temple of the living God and I take care of it properly. I watch everything that goes into my body or into my mind. I react positively to all that happens. I have no fears. Everything is in divine order. Nothing has hurt me in the past and nothing hurts me now.

I rest. I relax. I thank God for a body that can heal itself. New vitality comes to me now. All signs of my cold [or virus] now disappear and I am free and whole once more. All is well with my body. Thank God!"

Digestion

Whether we eat to live or live to eat, we have to be concerned with our digestion. Our intricate digestive system is a hardy one. It takes care of the good food and the not-so-good, the digestible and the indigestible. Much depends on our digestion: our disposition's affected as well as our general health. We know the things we should do to keep the digestive system harmonious.

We should eat the right foods in a happy atmosphere, taking time to chew our food well, being unhurried after eating, not worrying, not being tense. We know these things—but we don't always do them. We take our worries to the table with us. We gulp our food. We eat and run. We don't take time for regular elimination, we worry, we get depressed, we are full of fears, we hate things and people. We do all this and then wonder why we have indigestion, ulcers, liver upset, gallstones, constipation, appendicitis, diarrhea, and the rest. What can we do to heal the results of our unhealthy activity?

First we thank God for the wonderful system He

has created for us. We thank Him for all the involved processes, both mechanical and chemical, that go on without our knowing what is going on. We declare that divine order is getting things straightened out for us.

We take time now to remember the things we know we should do to keep the digestive system working in harmony. We start thinking and feeling as we should, for we are aware of the relationship between thoughts and emotions and digestion. We know better than we have done; now we start doing better. We help our actions by affirming:

"Everything in my body is functioning perfectly now. I am no longer depressed. I no longer fear anything or anybody. I no longer hate or worry. I am happy when I eat. If I am too tired or excited or upset, I delay eating until I have regained my composure. There is harmony, divine harmony, in my mind and emotions and in the operation of my body functions.

I select my food with care. I no longer push food into my mouth as if there were a time limit for eating. I control my appetite; it does not control me. I agree with my food and it agrees with me. All passageways are open and receptive to the food I am eating. I let go all restricting and binding thoughts. I take time for proper elimination of waste from my body. I eliminate old ideas, old habits that are not for my highest good. I keep my body clean inside and out. I exercise."

We make it easy for the purifying, cleansing, healing power to take care of whatever condition is present. We expect the healing, and it comes.

Drugs

The end of the world hasn't come if we find we are facing a drug problem. There are many in the world facing this kind of need for healing. But no problem is too big for us to handle intelligently and lovingly and successfully with God's help and direction.

Modern transportation, communication, and early wisdom of the world for our children all work together. From watching television, children know everything early; fast cars get them far and instantly away from supervision; they've been given everything or they've had nothing. Everything is geared high. It's no wonder when they reach out for recognition, group approval, for inspiration, to find themselves, that they use high-powered, dangerous ways. They don't think in small ways, they don't think in old ways.

Yes, man still has the same desires and needs, the same possibilities. He has the same needs for health of body and mind, for personal recognition of individual worth, for accomplishment, achievement, success, for ego satisfaction, for happiness, for love, for God. Man has always tried every way he could think of to get these things; too many of today's youth are trying drugs. They want wholeness, possibility, experience. They don't want to miss a thing. What we have to do is try to help them so they won't miss everything. We want them to have meaningful experiences, meaningful lives. The drug route to meaning, escape, recognition is being used by young people from every kind of background. For many it is one way to get attention.

For some from broken homes, for others who have known lack, for the unattractive, the poor achievers, drugs seem to offer a possible way to get attention they have never had. It is also a way to live dangerously, and young people have always dared, always wanted to try the unknown. They are searching for the reality of themselves which they hope to find through the thoughts and hallucinations that can come. They don't know and probably wouldn't admit that they are actually searching for the God within; they know there is a need, a yearning, an unsatisfied something inside, and maybe drugs are the answer.

For many young people drugs are the "in" thing, the door opener to "the group," the thing that shows which side of the gap they're on, the place where the action is. Undoubtedly for most, it's another way of experimenting, a contemporary way of looking at a flower or an insect or a blade of grass to find out what is, a taking-the-clock-apart-to-see-what-makes-it-tick, *a search to find out.*

If we can remember these things, remember how in our own way we too searched, did things that weren't wise as we experimented and searched, we won't panic when we discover a loved one is giving drugs a try, being with people we suspect are users. God is still in His heaven, in us, in our children, in the kids next door, down the street, on our campuses; we mustn't forget it, not for a minute.

We must not forget the difference between person and action. We deplore the action but we love the person. We let both the deploring and the love be known; we try to think with love, to trust with love, to speak with love, to do everything with love. We even worry with love! We never lose the faith, not for one minute. We give God the power, not the drugs. We try to understand what the need is, to know that with God's help we can fill that need. We know, above all, that this isn't final, that this too can pass, and that awful as it may seem, good can come through any experience, even when it is sordid, ugly, and legally wrong. We are especially careful not to do or say anything to invite resentment and defiance.

At the same time we make it clear that we know what it's all about, and that we don't like what we know. We praise and give thanks for every good thing, we try to find other ways of satisfaction; most of all, *we are there*—available, understanding, willing, expecting good to come, our faith in God so clear that we shine in the darkest moments.

We watch for the smallest indication of change or desire for change. We refuse to condemn; we try to help. We stand firm. We do not waver. We are there, the same yesterday, today, tomorrow, expecting good to come, listening for God's suggestion for ways to help. We believe in good in our young people no matter what they are doing or saying. The good is there and we help call it out by seeing it. We don't talk about specific young people, or young people in general, in disparaging ways. When we can, we express our optimistic hope for change for the better. Ideas will come.

One parent got the idea of writing letters to the angel of his son. When he was particularly disturbed by things the boy did and could find peace no other way, he talked out loud to the angel. This was the one way he was able to keep from condemning the boy and losing heart over a situation that seemed to get worse. Not only did he gain trust in the angel but he regained trust in the boy . . . for if the boy did have an angel with him (the God nature always with him) then he had to come out all right and couldn't be all bad. It kept the father from "worrying himself sick."

It worked out. The two were able, as the boy termed it, to "rap." Communication was restored. The boy found that his father really wanted to help him, that Dad knew more about drugs than he did and was ready to listen and try to change things that were bothering the boy. Above all, his father wanted him to bring his friends around, and had no condemnation of them either. The boy told him later, "Here I was about to split . . . " What he would have missed if he had taken off, unequipped for little but failure at the time!

Drug use was the latest in a list of unhappy experiences a mother had gone through with her daughter. The girl was very tall, not very pretty; she didn't do well in school, had no close friends, had a violent temper. She had cut out from school many times; she had trouble at some time every year, it seemed, with at least one teacher. Then she started running with a group known to be on dope. They were all involved in a police raid. Older ones were held for trial, the younger ones released on probation to their parents. The mother was appalled. It was some time before she could even pray calmly. When she did get still enough she started having ideas.

So often ideas we get in prayer time don't seem to make sense—but we'd better follow through. This mother did. At breakfast the next morning she asked the girl for some ideas on redecorating the living room. When the girl discovered that her mother was serious and wanted her ideas, no matter how different they might be, she became excited. They spent two weeks planning. The final plans sounded "way out" but the mother was game.

Some of the girl's new friends came by to help. The mother discovered that under the long hair, the combed and the uncombed, behind the fuzzy beards, were simply teen-agers, bright, more knowing than in her generation, but the same really. They still wanted the things she and her friends had: fun, people liking them, freedom to be.

The next idea came after more prayer: to give her daughter modeling lessons. This took care of the feeling of inferiority associated with the girl's height. Working together with paint brushes and rollers had helped her popularity. Knowing her mother cared for her and her associates bolstered the girl's feelings about herself, and many changes came about.

The girl became attractive, she had more friends, her grades improved. Some of the "group" dropped out of her life permanently, others stayed, and they too were helped by the mother.

Parents of a boy who had been experimenting with drugs (and who didn't know they knew) helped both themselves and him by using these statements:

"*You have divine judgment and you use it. You have divine perspective and you see things as they really are. No one fools you. You do not fool yourself. God is the only power in your life. He gives you divine wisdom and you use it in every thing you do. We love you and want the best for you now and always.*"

Emotions

Emotions are like people: we often don't know what to do with them but we know we can't do without them! We're in trouble if we don't have any emotional responses; we're in deep trouble if our responses are too many or too intense. Our involuntary system reacts to emotions; the good thing about them is that we can control them if we will. Our emotions don't have to turn us on; we can turn them on and we can turn them off. We can be selective. We must be, for we can mess up our life if we don't.

Emotions get into everything in our life. Our thinking is charged with emotion. Our vocabulary is studded with words of emotion. Our feelings and reactions are determined by emotions we have had. Our life is largely the result of emotions we have expressed and repressed. So many of our decisions, most of the big ones, are decided by our emotions.

We leave jobs because of our emotions, we get married to a certain person because of an emotion, we move sometimes because we can't get along with our neighborhood, we determine our social life by our emotions, we choose colleges and jobs very often because of emotional response. And most of us are emotionally sick—some of us only a little, others seriously, even critically.

We don't always call it emotional sickness; but when we react with instant prejudice, instant hate, anger, when we blow up at anything, when we are sensitive and our feelings get hurt all the time, when we become excited about anything and everything, when we are afraid of almost everything, when we jump to conclusions, we are being a little sick emotionally. When we jump on people we're really sick.

We know when we are emotionally sound and whole and well. We're happy, and we feel good everywhere. We get along with people, we do our work well, we have friends, we go places and we do things. We don't waste any time, effort, or strength on sick emotions. We don't let emotions happen. We aren't careless with our emotions.

We become conscious of things and people we are emotional about. We become objective. This makes it easier for us to know which emotions are hurting us physically or endangering our successful, happy living. We start encouraging the emotions that are making us healthier and happier and more effective. We take time to evaluate. We delay speaking or acting until we have separated emotional reaction from wise action. We cultivate a calm outlook on life and calm responses to everything that happens. It is not that we don't want emotion in our life; we want to be sure that the emotions we allow are the ones we want. Many techniques can help us.

One woman found that repeating this statement countless times a day helped her: *"I do not have to respond this second. I can wait a bit."* She felt better. She had fewer upset stomachs. There were fewer scenes at the dining table. Her days went better in every way.

A man who had what he thought was the most incompetent help in the world found that he had the best possible employees after he started using this affirmation constantly: *"Nothing matters in this office except my being kind and understanding."*

Fewer mistakes were made, no one dissolved into tears after one of his tirades. Absenteeism went down almost to zero.

One woman was amazed to find how emotional she really was. She had always thought of herself as being a beautifully controlled person. Instead she discovered that she was tense in holding back her emotional reactions. Her body was actually a tight criss-cross of nerves and muscles that rarely relaxed. The following helped her until she became what she wanted to be:

"With God's help I go easily through today. My body is relaxed, my mind is relaxed, my emotions are relaxed. I have a good sense of humor. I see things as they really are. I know that everything, every happening can be adjusted, repaired, changed, made right. I am flexible. I am open. I see things as they must appear to others, not just from my angle. I like people. I respond to what they do and say with kindly affection. I am no longer on the defensive. I put no one else on the defensive, for I am no longer critical or condemning. I am not even demanding. I let life happen. I take everything in my stride and my life is easy, happy, successful, harmonious, peaceful now. With God's help I can do this today."

We can decide what emotions we let loose in our life. We can decide how we want to respond and react. We are the deciders of our emotions. When we do the deciding, everything in our life improves.

Epidemics

We are all very susceptible to what others say and feel. Epidemics thrive on fear. Doctors and nurses can go through epidemics untouched, because they are not afraid. We don't have to be afraid either. We don't have to be caught in the stampede of mass thinking. We can come through epidemics untouched.

Constantly we have to come back to the basic question of our life: To what am I giving power? To God or to the epidemic? It is only after we are very sure of our position that we know there is nothing to fear in contamination, since God is all in all. We can stop epidemics if we know this, for always the truth we know for ourself we know for others. We can know for everyone else, whether they are aware of it or not, the one Power and the one Presence; and we can help them realize that the only power an epidemic has is the power given to it by expectation and fear. The only true infection is the infection of good.

Several years ago a mother with three small children was in the midst of a polio epidemic. Everywhere she went she was warned, people expressed fear for her children. She knew she had to get busy protecting them spiritually. She took good care of them physically, seeing that they had plenty of rest. She kept them away from other people—not from fear of infection but to keep the fear and notion of the epidemic out of their minds as much as possible. She refused to talk about polio to anyone. She thought of God's Presence. As she looked at her neighborhood, she saw the Presence there; as she drove through the city, she felt the Presence everywhere. She blessed every one she saw with the protective power of God, the same power she was calling on for her family.

She used the words of the 91st Psalm: "my Lord, 'my refuge and my fortress; my God, in whom I trust.' For he will deliver you . . . from the deadly pestilence; . . . You will not fear the terror of the night, . . . nor the pestilence that stalks in darkness."

She thought of this darkness as fear of the epidemic. As she was thinking, the words of an old hymn came to her mind: "Walking in the light, walking in the light."

We can all walk in the light. We can be protected as this little family was from fear, from any epidemic. When we read or hear about an epidemic of any kind anywhere we can know that those involved can walk in the light, can be free from fear, for God's presence is there more powerful than any epidemic.

A man found that this was true in a large office building when a virus epidemic seemed to take over. To symbolize the light he saw to it that blinds were not closed, that lights burned everywhere. He bought flowers, and said they were for the well. He thought of all his employees as happy, healthy, at work. He saw to it that there were new work ideas that kept the conversation away from the epidemic. He saw every one of his people in the Presence, walking in the light.

Not only was his office not "hit" as hard as the others in the building; the epidemic didn't last long anywhere.

This is a reminder to us to look away from appearances to healing and health. This is the way we walk in the light, stay in the Presence.

Fatigue

Many of us go to bed tired, wake up tired, feel we must have been born tired. We're tired in every part of us: in our muscles, in our bones. Our eyes feel tired. We never get caught up on sleep and we think we need something more than sleep to get over our fatigue.

What we need is to find our misplaced zest in living. We need to discover enthusiasm and joy, go to the Source for renewal of strength and energy. We need to remind ourself again who we are. As children of the Lord our strength comes from Him; and we can wait upon Him and have our strength renewed so that we can run and not be weary, walk and not faint.

Sometimes we carry a heavy mind and heart about with us, and nothing is more tiring. Do we carry our longtime hurts and disappointments around too? Are we happy? Joy and happiness lighten our work. If we will invite joy and happiness into our life, we will find that we are not "dead tired," we are alive, ready for the good of each day.

One woman who had been "tired for years" found

that she didn't have to be tired any longer after she started thanking God each morning: "*Today is filled with joy for me and mine. My tasks get done easily because I am so happy.*"

One woman said she overcame fatigue by forgetting how much there was to do and thinking only about the work in front of her. "The Lord provides for each moment," she said. This was enough to make the difference.

A man who could not remember when he hadn't felt tired tried these affirmations: "*God takes the drudgery out of my work. Help comes to me in many ways. My work load is lightened. My body gets completely rested. I am through with being so tired.*"

Help on his job came in unexpected ways. He got to the place where he went to bed because he was sleepy, and not because he was "dead tired."

No matter how long we have been fatigued, we can feel like a new person as we let joy and happiness come first into our mind and then into our work. It will go all through our body. We will find that we are walking with lighter footsteps, we are waking up eager to find what each day brings, we are expecting to be helped if we need to be, instead of expecting to be overworked. Our fatigue can be healed; our work can be accomplished without exhausting us.

Fever

Fever is part of the body's defense against disease. Fever indicates that the body is speeding up its attack on invaders, rushing lots of white cells to the scene of the attack, redoubling efforts to carry off waste substances. Metaphysically, fever indicates fear, worry, lack of harmony. It is these things we should be concerned about more than the fever.

Doctors too are much more concerned about the cause of fever than the thermometer reading itself. When we have fever we can take a moment to be grateful for the wonderful recuperative system we have, for God's life in us ready to renew and correct. Even at that moment the healing is going on. We hasten our healing when we recognize it. We take care of fear when we express our faith in the body's ability to heal without delay and without limit.

Fever can give us practice in overcoming fear, and we all need this. Fever strengthens our faith because every time we have more faith than fear, fever goes and faith grows.

A young woman had a high fever. She was frightened not only by the degrees recorded on her thermometer but also by the fact that she was alone in a strange city. Then she remembered who she was and, as she dozed off in a feverish sleep, she prayed: "*Dear Father, You are here. I am not alone. You're here. I'm all right.*" She knew, even in her semiconscious state, that she did not have to be concerned with fever, aloneness, or the business she was supposed to attend to the next day. Nothing but God mattered.

When she awakened, she was completely herself. She felt well, as if there had never been a fever. For a moment she forgot that she had been sick. Then she remembered, and was grateful for her healing.

Several members of a family were ill at the same time. The youngest, who was six at the time, awakened in the middle of the night very hot and achey. He was frightened. He wanted one of his parents, but he remembered before he called out that they were both sick. Then he remembered the last lines of *The Prayer of Faith: "I know no fear, for God and love and Truth are here."*

At first the child had to make himself say it, because his mind was so concerned about his discomfort. He kept saying it and shortly he went to sleep. His fever was gone in the morning. He might not have remembered it at all if his mother had not remarked how glad she was that he was not sick too.

Then he said, "I was, but I wasn't afraid, and the fever went away." Our fevers will go away too if we are not afraid and if we remember that God and love and Truth are ever with us, protecting, healing, making all well with us.

Glands

Sometimes we forget about our glands. It's a good thing they never forget about us, for they keep us going. They all work together to sustain our health. They protect us in so many ways: they regulate growth, adjust assimilation of food, store food, stimulate activity throughout the body. They blend emotions with physical and mental functioning to make a healthy, whole person. Our glands are busy, and sometimes they need help from us to continue their perfect work for us.

Since their role is functional we can use divine order to help them act efficiently. When they are in divine order they are producing their special hormones, feeding, adjusting, balancing, regulating the body.

One woman who had been told she must have part of her thyroid "shot" by x-ray worked with divine order and the gland responded perfectly. Her words were simple and direct:

"My thyroid is functioning perfectly. There is divine order in all its activity. There is no over-action, there is no lack of action, there is no sick action, there is only perfect, healthy action. Divine order is established not only in my thyroid but in all my other glands."

Parents of a child who was growing more rapidly than desired used divine order to slow down the pituitary. Their affirmation was:

"There is no over-activity in any part of John's body. Divine order sees to that. Divine order con-

trols his growth. It is as it should be. He grows at the right rate of progress. His body develops perfectly and at the right time. God is in charge of his growth."

They refused to worry or to keep looking for any change. The change came, and the growth rate slowed down to normal.

Always when we work with divine order, ideas come for us to do things that will help the situation—perhaps changes in diet or in our pattern of living. Our body responds to our loving attention; our glands seem to respond the quickest of all.

We do give thanks for this wonderful ductless glandular system. Divine order keeps it working perfectly.

Growths

Growths of any kind on our body frighten us. They also embarrass us. It is often difficult for us to do anything about them spiritually because they seem so permanent; they are not part of us, but there they are. When it comes to healing them, getting rid of them, they look like unconquerable mountains, but they're not. Many people have found that Truth dissolves growths as readily as it ends colds or takes the pain out of burns.

Metaphysically, growths indicate piled-up hurt

or sorrow or disappointment. We need to spend a little time (not too much) thinking back: what have we let build up inside us from the past? Is there something we have forgotten to forgive and forget? Is there a sorrow we have hugged to us so long that it has become a big, big part of us? Are there any memories that continue to grow and hurt?

Whenever we let unhappiness, resentment, disappointment stay around, they grow and ultimately cause trouble. We should get rid of these troublemakers fast, by encouraging the growth of other things. The only growth we want or need is spiritual; we actually want only to grow in kindness, understanding, love, intelligence, wisdom. When we concentrate our growing on these things, other things get no nourishment or encouragement from us.

A woman had a small lump on one breast. Her doctor advised immediate surgery. She did not want surgery but wanted to use the Truth she was learning. Understandably, her family was concerned and agreed with the doctor. She did not resist, she let plans be made; but at the same time, she worked to know the Truth about herself—that she was truly the child of God, free from blemish, free from any growth except the spiritual. She worked metaphysically to know that healing was possible.

The lump got smaller. The doctor admitted it when she went for presurgery examination, but he and the family urged her to have the operation so that she wouldn't "run any chance." Healing was quick, and there has been no recurrence.

In a similar incident both doctor and patient decided to wait a little longer to see if the shrinking of the lump was permanent. It was. In both cases healings of the physical came as each woman healed emotional "growths." Each realized that she had an emotional hangup from past experiences.

Another woman used a simple statement: "*I expect a miracle, a miracle of healing today.*" She really had two miracles of healing,—one of the growth on her body, the other of feeling that she had been an unwanted child.

A man who had a growth on the back of his neck wanted it gone. It was a bother; every now and then the barber nicked it, and it didn't seem to heal rapidly. In his metaphysical reading, the man had seen the term "spiritual surgery." This he thought could be the right answer to his growth. He liked the sound of it. He prayed that spiritual surgery would take place and remove the growth:

"*Remove from me, dear Father, not only this lump that has bothered me so long but also whatever else in me needs to go. I'm ready. I release old animosities, old fears, old hurts. I don't want them. I want to be free from anything that interferes with my spiritual progress or that is detrimental to my physical well-being.*"

He had a dream a few nights later about going through actual surgery for removal of the neck growth. The dream was still vivid in his mind when he awakened, and he hurried to look in the mirror. The lump was gone. He did not know what emotional "growth" he had also eliminated from his subconscious. It didn't matter. His neck was smooth again, with only a slight indentation that quickly filled in. He was jubilant.

What these people did we can do too. We can desire growth in grace and spiritual understanding;

we can eliminate negative emotional "growths"; we can expect the miracle of spiritual surgery.

Headaches

When our head aches, we're not good for much of anything except to suffer. We can't think straight. We don't feel like being pleasant. We're miserable. The ache gets between us and everybody and everything else. We can't think of anything else. After we've softened the ache a bit with a nap or a pill or a prayer, we wonder what caused it: tension, anxiety, faulty elimination, something we ate, worry? At the time, we don't care, we only want the headache to go away.

We need to have our headaches relieved for good, not just for now. We start inquiring about metaphysical reasons, and ways Truth can help. One cause given is an emotional spree; others are emotional shock interfering with digestion, resentment, mental habits that interfere.

Did something so upset us that we really did go into a tailspin? Are we so tense that we've been "blowing our stack"? Have we been so hurt that we cried, or wanted to? Maybe we did have an emotional spree and this is the hangover, the morning after; maybe this is the starting place for us to change things:

"My emotions are balances. I go on no emotional sprees. I react peacefully, calmly. I know that I do not have to get upset over anything. I know that all things can be taken care of, ironed out, so I 'keep my cool'. God's healing power is now taking care of my emotional hangover. Whatever caused this headache is gone. I give myself to God and He takes care of me."

We help the situation by taking care of our body better, by watching our emotions. We study our headaches, becoming more aware of what we think and do before one of them starts. This way we have a better chance to know what is "bugging" us and to take care of it.

Jake was a law student who got a terrible headache nearly every time he had an exam. It lasted about two days every time. At first he thought maybe deep inside he was afraid of the exam, but that wasn't it. The headache was caused by his mental turmoil in trying to get ready for the test. Not only was he mentally confused and worried, he was resentful that there was so much to review, so little time. His head rebelled. Finally Jake saw to it that with God's help he could be one with God's Mind and know what to study and how:

"I am one with Divine Mind. I know what to study and how to study. I understand, I remember, I think clearly, I express myself well on my examination. My help comes from God."

Deadlines, closing sales, interviews can all be emotional sprees if we are not careful, leaving headaches as an aftermath. The wonderful part about spiritual healing is that both cause and effect are taken care of at the same time:

"I take things calmly. I do things I have to do without getting all worked up. I do not waste my emotional power. I use my feelings for good only. I no longer waste my physical strength on needless emotional reactions. My head is free from aches and pains. My headaches are now gone, praise God!"

Hearing

It can be dangerous not to hear clearly. Misunderstandings come when we do not hear exactly what other people say to us. We miss a lot, and we don't want to miss a single good thing. So we start thinking about hearing from a spiritual point of view.

We check to see what we are hearing, what we are listening to. Are we hearing God noises or only negative people noises? Are we listening to hear God speak through people, speak through nature? Do we hear God speak when we are given instructions to carry out?

A man had been "hard of hearing" for as long as he could remember. He wore a hearing aid and it helped, but he wanted freedom from having to wear it. He also wanted to be sure he was hearing everything he was supposed to hear. He thought of the healing touch of Jesus Christ, His healing words. He thought of his own spiritual selfhood, made in the image and likeness of God. As a son of God, he knew he should have all the abilities of the Father. He should have perfect hearing.

This was an exciting idea to him. Something stirred inside him and wouldn't let him rest until he did something to start the healing processes going. There was a growing feeling that he would actually be able to hear again. It was very exciting.

He kept thinking about it and he kept listening for God everywhere. He listened for God through others, and he found he understood and liked people better. He listened to the birds, and he learned more about them. It seemed he could even hear what the flowers were saying, the rush of air, the movement of branches and leaves. Whenever he was asked to do something, he said silently: *"God is asking me. God is speaking to me. I hear Him. I hear Him in all things now."*

He continued to be excited, yet he wasn't in any hurry. Time didn't seem to count. It seemed that *the healing had already taken place,* so what was there to hurry about? He really had been hearing things that he had never heard before, or even thought of listening to hear. Then it happened.

At first he was a little irritated. He was hearing so many scratchy noises. He thought he had turned his hearing aid up too high. Then he remembered: he didn't have the hearing aid on. The batteries had run down and he had to get new ones. *He was hearing!* He dropped down on his knees to thank God. Even though he had never doubted that his prayers would be answered, it was a little overwhelming when the healing became complete.

Another man had an injury and was told that his

hearing was permanently impaired. He refused to accept this verdict. He used these statements as his preparation for a spiritual healing: "*There is nothing too difficult for God to repair. He is healing me, restoring my hearing, making me hear perfectly now. I hear perfectly now. The healing has already taken place. I praise and give God thanks for His healing work in my body.*"

He persisted in his prayers, refusing to think that anything except healing would take place. His faith in spiritual healing never once wavered. His hearing was restored.

Heart

Publicity and statistics keep us aware that we must take care of our heart physically and emotionally—but spiritual care is the fundamental care we must give our wonderful heart. We know physical strain and overwork can damage our heart; we know emotions can. When we get excited or angry, our heartbeats become very rapid. If we are afraid, this happens, too; also when we are very, very happy. Sometimes we forget that the heart is a muscle and needs exercise (but not too much at a time). There are many ways for us to help our heart do its vital work for us.

We can appreciate our heart more, praise it, be proud that we have such a marvelous mechanism within us. We can listen to our heartbeats and know that they are beautifully planned to be steady, regular—a beat, then a rest, then a beat. This can cue our activity. We work or exercise; we rest; we work or exercise. Our heartbeats have a rhythm keeping us in harmony with the rhythm of the universe.

One woman who had a dangerously rapid heartbeat with attendant conditions found that her heart responded to this truth that she used as a basis for her affirmations: "*I am in harmony with the universe. My heart beats in perfect rhythm with the rhythm of the world. It beats steadily, regularly, slowly, wonderfully, perfectly, joyfully. My heart is filled with love and love regulates my heart, heals it, repairs it. God is in my heart. Love is in my heart. My heart expresses health and love and life. Thank God!*"

Another woman, who had dropsy, found that similar statements took care of the accumulation of liquid in her legs and abdomen and restored her heart health: "*There is perfect flow of liquids in my body; there is no stoppage or interference with any function. My heart is perfect. It expresses only healthy conditions. I listen happily to the regular, steady, rhythmic beat of my heart, and I rejoice. Divine love and order are in control of all my body functions and I am made well and whole.*"

Both women kept healing in mind—not the condition that the heart was in at the time. There was no fear, no worry, only the certainty that the healing was taking place.

Another woman who loved to dance used a

musical beat affirmation to help her body heal her heart. *"Love, love, love,"* she said over and over with the beats of her heart. *"Peace, peace, peace. Health, health, health. Steady, steady, steady. Order, order, order. Love, love, love, and peace, peace, peace."* Often the repetition lulled her to sleep. When she walked she regulated her pace, using the same words and the same tempo.

A man with an enlarged heart knew that his heart was big only with love, that the physical organ was its perfect normal size, and that all of his heart's actions were perfect and as they should be.

"My heart is big with love. My heart is filled with love. My heart beats with love. My heart sends love out through my body. My heart is healed with love. My heart is made perfect by love."

It's good to work with love. Sometimes it seems hearts get in trouble because they are literally aching for love. They feel lack of love. This may be a lack of love from a certain person, or simply a lack. It may well be (whether it is so recognized at first or not) a lack of awareness of God's love. It is difficult for most of us to comprehend God's love. We think, "Who are we that God should love us?" And it's hard to accept the fact that He loves us with an everlasting love. But often hearts get well when their owners start to feel God's love.

One young woman who had had a most unhappy adolescence found that each time she said, *"God loves me, God loves me,"* she was better. Another young person received healing help simply by thinking of Jesus Christ and all the love He expressed. He had never seemed closer to her nor her healing so possible as when she searched for proofs of His expression of love. Studying His life and work, she began to feel a wondrous love within her. This love changed her life.

She felt different about everybody and everything in her life. Her body felt different. There was new life and vitality through every part, including her heart, which soon became normal. She still uses the affirmations that came to her as she thought about Jesus and His love:

"The love of Jesus Christ is in me now. I feel it, I express it. It heals me. It makes me strong."

Infection

Sometimes the smallest cut will get infected. Often hurt places fail to heal properly because of infection. Sometimes we get sick because of infection. How do we go about healing infection spiritually?

One woman with a badly infected hand did it this way: *"I am not susceptible to any infection except spiritual infection,"* she affirmed. *"I want to be spiritually infected. I want to be infected with love, wisdom, intelligence, life, strength. There is no infection except spiritual infection. I am thankful that this is so."*

Her hand was healed overnight.

Another person visualized the healing white light of the Christ in the part of her body that was infected. She made a game of seeing the white light instead of the swollen, blotchy, red skin. As she watched and thought about the white light, it seemed that it spread and went all through her body. (We can train our inner eyes to see the healing process as readily as we can let them see only the present physical condition.) As she watched, she said over and over to herself:

"The healing white light of the Christ is eradicating all infection. It heals as it touches. It leaves perfect healing wherever it is and it is all through my body now. Thank God for this powerful healing light. It is the light that was in Jesus Christ."

Within a few hours the swelling had gone down, and very shortly after that all indications of any infection were gone too.

Infection can frighten us; we must be very sure that we are less afraid of the infection than we are sure of its healing. We need to make certain that we are not judging by appearances. It is understandable to be startled and concerned by flesh appearances, but we can get to the place where they do not bother us at all. We know only that here is an opportunity for us to let God's healing power work again in us. It helps if we declare:

"No physical appearance disturbs me. I see beyond appearances to perfect healing. This infection has no power. God is the power in me and for me, the only power in me and for me. His healing power is taking care of this appearance and this dis-ease now. I help the healing process by not being disturbed. There is nothing to fear, there is nothing

to be disturbed about. God is in complete charge. The healing is being done now. Praise God!"

A man always felt the warmth of the love of the Christ. When there was need for healing of a foot infection he concentrated this feeling of warmth on his foot: *"The warmth of the love of Jesus Christ heals my foot now. There is only comfort and ease in it now."*

He said that he could almost feel the warmth "driving out" the infection. He was comfortable in a few minutes, and the infection kept getting less and less until it was completely gone.

Insomnia

It's not the occasional night of sleeplessness that concerns us seriously; a good night's sleep the next night, and we're as good as new. It's the night after night after night of not sleeping that needs our healing thought.

Sleeplessness breaks the rhythm of waking and sleep, and it is hard on the body. While we sleep the repair work of the body goes on twice as fast as it does during our waking hours. We need to make all our nights good, restful ones and we can. We can help by not worrying about not sleeping!

Sleepless minutes or hours are wonderful opportunities for us to do more metaphysical work. It is easier for us to meditate in the stillness of a sleeping household; there are no outer interruptions. It is an opportunity too for us to read, to study and, above all, to do prayer work for other people. If we spend our sleepless time this way we will be accomplishing something; if we roll and toss and worry about not sleeping, we only tire ourself more. Praying, meditating can help get us back in rhythm with sleep. Sleepless hours can be profitable hours when we fill them with prayer and metaphysical study.

One man got the idea that it didn't matter whether or not he slept. He had a growing business and there were many decisions to make. For more than a month he had slept very little. As his fatigue increased, his tension increased and he was even less able to sleep at the end of the month. He was doubly bothered. He needed all his strength and his "wits about him." He needed a clear, rested mind in order to make the most of opportunities open to him. The decisions he had to make were important because he would be living with them for a long time.

Only one night's sleep could make the difference, he felt. One night would break the train of sleepless nights. As he prayed he got the impression that it didn't matter at all whether he went to sleep or stayed awake. "All right, God," he said. "Maybe I don't need sleep. I'm going to take Your word for it. I'll stop being concerned about it. You take over. You give me the sleep You think I need. I'm in Your hands and I know everything will be all right."

Releasing the concern about insomnia snapped his tension and, almost before he had thought the words of his prayer of acceptance, he was asleep. He still puts himself in the Father's hands each night, because the sleep he got that night was more restful than any sleep he had ever had.

One woman got back in rhythm with sleep by going to sleep whenever she felt sleepy, no matter what time of day it was or what she was doing. She said only, "Thank You, Father," as she dropped down on the nearest bed or couch. At first she didn't even take off her shoes. Not all of us can go to sleep at any time of the day because of our work and responsibilities, but we can say "Thank You, Father" each night as we get into bed and settle ourself for the night.

For the first time in her life a woman was living alone. She was all right during the day but at night she was frightened. Everything seemed different at night, even with the lights on. She was afraid to go to sleep. She tried to read but every little noise made her jump. She thought of finding someone to live with her, but she didn't really want that. Most of all, she didn't want to be afraid, and she wanted to be able to go to bed and go to sleep every night.

She prayed for an answer, prayed to know what could bring her fearless sleep. The answer came so clearly that it was as if Someone had spoken aloud to her: "*You are never alone. I am with you. I am with you now. I am with you always. I watch over you always. You can sleep knowing that I am watching over you, every minute of every night. There is no need for you to be afraid. I am here.*"

She had forgotten (as all of us do at times) that God is "nearer than breath, nearer than hands." Her fear was completely gone. Her insomniac nights were over.

Lungs, Breathing

We are more conscious today of our lungs than we once were, with all the talk about the dangers of smoking, of smog, of cancer. We are reading and thinking about respiratory diseases; we know what emphysema is. (A few years ago, not many of us had even heard of it.) We have known about breathing for good health, and we have known about the breath of life. Not often did we connect the two ideas. We are starting to do so now.

Body health depends on continuous intake of air. The body can get along without food for several days, water for a shorter length of time. Air it must have all the time. And before we can really live, we have to understand that we can breathe in life. This what some call *prana,* others *mana,* others the renewing, revitalizing, energizing, healing power of God. We have to become aware of this breath of life before we can use it for maximum benefit. When we consciously breathe in Life, *prana, mana,* we get the full good from it. We find it heals, relaxes, strengthens, purifies. It helps us in our prayer and meditation.

We need to breathe in this vital breath, gently and deeply, when we start our prayer time. If we are disturbed or too active mentally we can quiet ourself by breathing very gently, keeping our mind on the inflow of life-bringing air and the outflow of the air that carries off not only body waste but everything and anything that is disturbing us. By breathing deeply and filling all of our air capacity, we become healthier, happier, yes, nicer. Dispositions improve with good breathing habits.

One woman, who discovered that she had been breathing only with the top of her lungs, found that it helped her remember to breathe deeply and also (which was even more vitally important) that she was breathing in the very breath of God, the breath of Life and restoration and renewal, when she said mentally: *"I breathe in God, I breathe in good. I breathe out everything that I no longer need, that is no longer good for me to hold."* This helped her to breathe deeply, gently, and rhythmically.

A man used a similar technique. When he was very tired, he took a few slow, deep breaths, saying to himself as he inhaled, *"I breathe in rest, renewal, vitality, energy,"* and as he exhaled: *"I breathe out fatigue. I breathe out all tiredness."* If he was angry, he breathed out his disturbed feelings and breathed in peace. If he was afraid, he breathed in courage, faith, assurance and breathed out fear. It always worked for him.

As we breathe we can send the healing breath of life to all our body, through all our respiratory system, to any diseased or hurting part of our body. A woman directed the healing breath to a burned hand, and the healing was miraculously fast. A man who had not been able to overcome the smoking habit used the healing breath to cleanse him of all desire to smoke and to cleanse his body of all residue from the long years of smoking.

Another man found that it helped him get over the difficult period to get up from work when the desire came to smoke and go outside (or to another room) and take several slow, deep breaths.

A man with emphysema had read about a doctor

who had helped people with respiratory diseases by teaching them deep breathing. He decided to try it. He had been miserable since he had to give up smoking. When he started the deep, slow breathing coupled with stretching and bending exercises, it helped him overcome the deep-seated desire to smoke. It also healed him of emphysema. With each breath he breathed in healing, new life, replenishing of vitality and energy. He breathed out all thought of weakness and disease.

We breathe in life, we breathe in God's healing power, we breathe in new life, new energy. We breathe out everything that is unlike God in our life, our body, and our experiences. We are healed now and we stay healed, whole, healthy, perfect.

Malformations

Nothing is impossible with God. "If you can! All things are possible to him who believes." *All things,* not just some things, are possible. We have to remember this in any healing work we do; we have to remember it constantly when we are working for healing of a malformation. It takes true belief, real faith when there is part of the body that is not formed perfectly. It is one of the most difficult conditions for us to handle because it is so hard for us to see the perfect formation and pay no attention to the present appearance. When we can, when we really believe, miraculous things happen.

A teen-age boy had one leg that had always been twisted. When he got the idea of the possibility of healing, he never wavered in his belief: "*My leg can be healed by the God power in it. I see my leg perfect and straight as it should be. The straightening comes about without delay. Thank God for this healing now.*"

He made himself walk more, farther, faster. He did ankle exercises, he stretched, he bent, he jogged, he ran. All the time he thanked God for the healing. His leg did straighten so that he could use it much more freely than he ever had.

A young woman had injured her elbow when she was twelve. She had not been told to exercise the arm after her cast was removed. She had accepted the misshapen elbow, which was larger than the other one. Then she accepted the idea that with God all things are possible, and she prayed for direction and for healing. Ideas came. She started exercising the elbow even though it was almost too stiff to move at all. She rubbed it and her arm with warm oil before she exercised and afterward. All the time she looked at her "good" elbow and tried to picture the other as free-moving and beautiful.

It was not easy. Often she had to say out loud: "*I do believe, I do believe. I do believe that this elbow can be changed.*" Improvement came slowly, but it came. Her body responded as the body always does to praise and loving, expectant attention.

When we notice improvement, we hasten healing. Our praise calls the healing forth and it comes much more rapidly. It also helps us look more confidently to healing and helps break the mesmerism of the malformation. It takes diligence to erase from our mind the picture of the condition. We often have to break the spell of time.

Time meant nothing to the Christ in His healing ministry. We try to follow Him in all things, and we must in this. We do not give time any power in our life when a healing is needed. We do not think that one condition is any more difficult than another to heal, even though it has been with us longer. We change our thinking by looking to a healing and expecting it to come.

A woman had swollen, stiff joints on three fingers. She used this affirmation and healing came: "*All stiffness, pain, soreness, discomfort give way to the healing spirit of Your joy, dear Father. My fingers are perfect as You made them. Thank You.*"

A man had a toe that was stiff; it hurt when it touched the end of his shoe. His successful healing thought was: "*Love, divine love, transforms all my body including my toe. It is no longer stiff and it doesn't hurt. My body is whole and perfect. I praise and thank God for His healing power at work in my body right now.*"

Mental Health

We all want to be whole—physically, mentally, and emotionally. Each part of us must be healthy if all of us is to be. Our mental stability can be upset by physical or emotional dis-ease. Shock, emotional or physical stress can make us mentally ill. Mental disturbance can make us physically ill. Any one or any combination of these can affect us in varying degree. Whether our mental ill health is mild or severe, it is always marked by reactions to life and by behavior that is exaggerated in some way—either inappropriate to the situation or not acceptable as normal. Regardless of the type of mental sickness or its seriousness, health and healing are possible. As with physical illness, the length of time that the condition has existed does not matter so far as the possibility for healing is concerned. Mental healing is possible regardless of time.

We know Jesus Christ healed mental unrest. We know what Paul told us to do to become mentally healthy: "be transformed by the renewal of your mind." *Renewal of the mind is the hope held out for healing mental sickness.* Renewal of the mind makes mental wholeness possible, even when it can seem to human understanding and to all appearances impossible.

A man had gone through severe mental depression. He had had a long series of shock treatments. His family had been told that he would never be "much more than a vegetable"; however, he would not likely be a dangerous problem to himself or to them. He looked terrible; he knew it and he didn't want anyone to see him. When visitors came, he went off by himself or sat far back in the room. He read his Bible every now and then. One day his eyes caught Paul's words.

They made the first real impression on him that anything had since before his shock treatments. As he said later, those words were like a tiny light in a dark, dark night. When there is no light at all, a tiny brightness can be very big. This light was bright enough to start him praying for the first time since he became depressed. At first he prayed only, "*Renew my mind.*" Then another candle was lighted and he asked, "*Transform my body; transform my mind.*" Then he asked for renewal of the body. Gradually there was a transformation, renewal of both mind and body.

Effects of the shock treatments disappeared; his body was healthy. He didn't look the same, he didn't act the same, he certainly didn't think the same. He achieved normal mental health. So did a young woman who was so depressed after the birth of a child that she tried three times to kill herself.

A relative was the channel for her healing. Not once did he accept her depression as more than a passing condition. Not once did he think or say that there was no hope for her. Often mental healing has to start with a person who cares. The healer never loses sight of the whole person, the whole personality. He always knows that healing can and will come. He never becomes discouraged no matter how long it takes for the healing to be complete.

His strength, his faith can be the first strength for the patient. So often the mentally sick need this reassurance of someone who cares enough to believe in the possibility of healing. Doctors, psychiatrists know this too; if their patients are aware of a truly caring interest plus sureness of the possibility of recovery, the healing is more rapid and permanent.

When Paul wrote to the Corinthians, he told them, "we have the mind of Christ." These words were the constant prayer of a mother whose son went through a severe mental illness. Over and over and over again she repeated these words.

At first her heart had been so heavy that she was not able to think that there could be a change in her son. But these words healed her thoughts. If he had the mind of Jesus Christ, he could certainly be healed, be whole and sound again. Her thoughts went on to the possibility that if this were so, then there would not have to be months or years of therapy and treatment. The words stayed with her day and night. When she went to sleep they comforted her; when she awakened they gave her strength for the day.

Soon she had the courage to use them to him: "*You have the mind of Christ.*" Every time she thought of the Christ she saw Him in a bright light glowing with health, strength, and beauty. She was soon thinking and seeing her son in the same way. One day she told him this. He looked at her for a long time, then he said quietly, "If I have the light of the Christ and the mind of Christ, I'm not sick at all."

After that they were able to declare together: "*I have the mind of Christ. I am surrounded by the white light of the Christ and I am completely healed.*"

We too have the Christ mind. This heals us, guides

us, protects us, instructs us. There is healing in the words.

Muscles

What a complexity of muscles we are! Often we are conscious only of the larger muscles. It is difficult to comprehend that there are, for instance, six hundred and twenty voluntary muscles as well as all the involuntary ones. They are a lesson for us in their wonderful coordination: no muscle works alone.

Despite the fact that every muscle is partially contracted all the time, constant tension hurts. Steady tension prevents waste products in the muscle from being removed continuously, and this is necessary to maintain muscle health. Muscles respond to nerve stimuli so they too work together. It is through this beautiful cooperation that our strength and energy come.

Perhaps we have so many muscles so that we can have unlimited strength in every part of our bodies. Strength has always been recognized as vital. Often in the Bible strength is coupled with the Lord, given as one of His attributes even as love, wisdom, goodness. "The Lord is my strength and my shield"; "God is our refuge and strength"; "The Lord is my strength and my song." There are many reminders of where our strength comes from and where we can go to get strength.

When we know and remember this, we remove the primary cause of muscle distress: strain. Fear of lack of strength adds strain to muscles. When we know that there is an unlimited source of strength from God, we do not have to strain. Actually we determine how much of the life and energy of God we use. We determine whether or not our muscles are helped by our drawing on the reserve power of God, to which we can have access through our thoughts and words.

A man who had worried his shoulder muscles stiff found healing only after he let his burden of thoughts go. He prayed to know that it was not his strength that was needed to do what he had to do, but God's strength. "*I do not have to carry all this work load myself. You will help me,*" he prayed. "*I can relax, let go. My strength is in the Lord, not in my physical body.*" His shoulder muscles relaxed, his worrying ceased. He had never felt more able to do things. He got much more done than he ever had before.

A woman had such severe pain in her muscles that she took strong muscle relaxants and pain deadeners. She wanted to be free from the necessity of taking the drugs. When she thought about the idea of her strength not being limited to her physical body but unlimited, because she could call on God's strength, she formulated the following statements that made the difference:

"*My muscles are healed as I let them go and let God's strength fill every one of them with new life and vitality. The Lord's strength flows into every muscle of my body, every big muscle and every little one. They all respond with health. My pain is gone. My tension is gone. I move freely all through my body."*

Her muscle elasticity returned. She was free to move and to do as she wanted to.

We are free from any binding. God's strength is ours now and forever.

Nerves

We have not one communications system in our body, but three: the central system, which has to do with whatever we consciously do or feel; the autonomous, with our involuntary actions (breathing and other automatic body functions); and the peripheral, which connects the extremities with the central system. We think with the whole body. We sense with the whole body. We feel with the whole body. This explains why we hurt all over, why our actions are all affected, when we have sick nerves.

It is our nerves that are affected when we are anxious, upset, lose our cool and our poise. It is our nerves that get tied up when we stop being relaxed and become tense.

A man who had had business losses started suffering from "old-fashioned neuralgia." There seemed to be pain in every nerve in his body. Inflammation of the nerves (neuritis) increased his discomfort. While trying to ease his pain, he tried to keep from using his arms. They became thin and stiff.

At times it seemed the pain rolled over his body in waves. He tried to take his mind off the pain and difficulty of movement by reading the Bible. His healing started when he read with fresh understanding Psalm 107, verses 28-30:

"Then they cried to the Lord in their trouble, and he delivered them from their distress; he made the storm be still, and the waves of the sea were hushed. Then they were glad because they had quiet, and he brought them to their desired haven."

To him these verses told his story: he was crying out to the Lord in his trouble. He believed that the Lord could bring him out of the real distress that he felt, although he didn't know how. He wanted the Lord to calm his nerves; he was ready to be glad because his nerves were quiet. He certainly wanted to come into a haven of health and healing.

He continued to think of his body as in a storm. He pictured the calm coming. Within a few hours he had relief, although he was not actually expecting it. It was a greater relief than any sedative gave him. In a short time he had complete freedom from nerve pain and tension.

Another man felt the healing in *"Peace, my peace, I give unto you."* He pictured the Christ saying this to him, saying it to every nerve in his body. Soon he felt his nerves respond to the command to be at peace. The relaxation was so complete that he slept for the first time without medication. The perfect and complete healing came without delay.

We can visualize healing in many ways when we have a need for the healing of nerves. Prayer with feeling is more effective than prayer without feeling. Prayer with visualized results adds to the feeling and the potency of our prayers. The visualization helps us feel and know and be thankful for the healing even before it manifests in the body.

The peace of Jesus Christ is poured out upon me and I am healed of all tension and pain. My nerves are quiet and receptive to His healing peace.

Pain

When we hurt, it is hard to be thankful for the pain. We should be, for pain is a warning signal to us that something in our body needs attention and healing.

When we bless pain, we take the worst hurt out of it. Blessing always changes things; blessing pain changes it. Often it stops the pain completely; it has for many people. Sometimes blessing gives an idea of the right thing to do to take care of whatever is causing the pain. Sometimes blessing relaxes us—and pain depends on tension. When we bless, we start relaxing, we start putting the pain on the defensive. Sometimes pain is only a warning, and blessing it helps us understand the warning.

It may be simply a warning for us to stop, to be

quiet, to give our body a chance to catch up with all that we are trying to have it do.

A man had deep, sharp pains around his eyes. He felt certain that his vision was all right. He didn't think he had been straining his eyes except (and this thought came to him as he was blessing the pain) that he *had* been feeling pressure to keep ahead of the work of a group of men whose activities he directed.

"God," he said, "are You trying to tell me to stop, to be still? Is this pain only a signal?" He went on that assumption. He stayed in bed one day in a darkened room. He tried not to think except to bless the pain and his eyes, and everything in his life. He slept. He woke up and the pain was not as severe. He slept again. The pain was gone when he awakened this time. He got up and went for a long walk, something he hadn't done for many, many months. When he returned he knew that he was free from a lot of pressures.

A woman had post-operative pain. She too blessed the pain and her body. She realized that the body does not approve of surgery; she knew that many muscles and nerves as well as tissue and blood vessels had been cut. Everything in her body was working overtime to heal her. She spent a great deal of her waking hours appreciating the wonders of her body, telling it she understood why it was complaining, blessing it for its healing work. That night she slept without sedation; the pain was gone. Her healing progressed rapidly.

I bless this pain. It is a stop signal. I relax. I listen for ideas. I do what I can to make my body comfortable, my mind at ease, and the pain goes. Thank God!

Paralysis

We are always frightened when we can't move freely. We don't want our body unable to move as we want it to or need it to. If we have a problem of constriction of movement, of paralysis, we have to remove the fear first. (We also have to do this if we are trying to help someone else who is facing this challenge.) We have to insist to ourself that freedom of movement is possible, that our real self can move now as it should, and then we get ready to be free. We are no longer afraid in our mind, we no longer allow ourself to think in terms of paralysis, we get ready for healing.

A woman awakened in the middle of the night feeling "funny." She was also very sleepy, so she said, "*God, You are taking care of me now,*" and went back to sleep. She had strange dreams. In each dream she was tied with a rope so that she couldn't move; in each dream she was in a different place and with different people.

In the morning she awakened lying on her right side, and she could not move the arm or leg under her. She smiled at first, thinking she was still experiencing her dream. Then she thought, "Maybe the dreams are telling me something." Then she became frightened.

She spoke sharply to herself mentally: "You asked God to take care of you last night. Are you thinking now that He can't? You have no business being scared. God has protected you many times. He will see you through this, whatever it is."

Her fear left. Once again she went back to sleep, thinking, "*God, You take care of me now.*"

She still could not move when she awakened, but she was not afraid. She remembered God first, not fear. Cautiously she pulled herself over with the muscles on her left side. Finally she was able to sit up. Each time she moved, she said: "*My body is free to move as it should. It is free, free, free. It moves as it needs to move. There is no binding of any muscle, no shutting off of any nerves.*" After some time and effort she was able to reach the telephone and call a friend who also believed that spiritual healing is possible in all conditions. For three days they continued to pray, blessing her body, knowing that she was free to move, that a perfect healing was taking place. By the fourth day all of her body moved freely. All that remained of the experience was a heaviness in her arms and legs. This too soon passed.

A man healed facial paralysis by using these prayer statements: "*Whatever needs to be done to bring life and vitality to my facial muscles is being done now. All of my body is in harmony with life. There is no debility in my body anywhere. Everything is alive, functioning in the way it should. God is healing me now, right now.*"

He exercised the facial muscles that were free and kept trying to move the others. He was not afraid. He trusted God for a healing. He did everything he could think of to build his body up. He knew God's life flowed through him without hindrance. He knew there were no clogged blood vessels, no injured blood vessels that could not be repaired. His healing came.

I am not afraid. Appearances do not scare me.

God moves through my body now and my body moves. I have perfect freedom of movement. Every part of my body moves freely now. Praise God!

Poisoning

There are many ways our bodies can be poisoned. The body refuses certain foods, the skin reacts to certain substances. If this occurs we do not panic, we do not get frightened. We remain calm, knowing that God is directing the life force in us, that if we are still enough to hear He will let us know what we should do to take care of the situation.

Then we remember about antidotes, we know what human steps to take. If we remain poised and calm, we will not make the poison a god; we will know that our God is more powerful than any poison can be.

A child swallowed some cleaning fluid. He and his mother were home alone, without transportation to go for help. The boy became still, as she instructed, for he had complete faith in his mother and in God. He listened carefully to all she said about God and healing. He listened in spite of his discomfort. Almost at once the child vomited several times. Then he asked for milk. The first drink came back up, but the next stayed down. Then he said he felt fine and wanted to go out to play. His mother thanked God for this wonderful healing.

Another child had fallen into a bed of poison ivy. When he got to his mother he was red and swollen over much of his body. His eyes were almost closed and his skin itched and burned. He was angry with the ivy that was the cause of his hurt. He cried and complained. His mother bathed him in heavy suds, washed carefully around his eyes, washed his hair, all the time telling him that he must get still.

"Your body cannot get calmed down," she told him, "until you are. God's healing power cannot work in you while you yell and are so angry. We mustn't blame the ivy. It tries to tell us to be careful by having always the same number of leaves. Do you remember the story of Jesus telling the stormy winds to be still when the disciples were so afraid in the boat?"

The boy remembered. He knew his body was in a storm. He tried to tell it to be still and he started feeling better. He wasn't very still, but because he tried, the healing started. This is all we ever have to do: try to think, say, believe what we can at the moment. As he realized how much better he was feeling, he said, "Thank you, mother." He was really thanking God, for she was God's channel of healing. Practically all indication of the poisoning was gone the next day.

God's healing power cleanses my body of any poisonous substance. I do not have to be afraid. My body with God's help gets rid of the poison now. I am healed right now. Thank God!

Seizures

Seizures

It can be a startling experience to be around a person when a seizure occurs. It is a shocking experience for the person who suffers one. This fear and shock must be healed first. Peace, the wonderful, healing peace of Jesus Christ, must be called on immediately. Body and mind of the victim, mind and emotions of the onlooker must be made still, hopeful, sure of healing as quickly as possible.

One man found this kind of healing necessary when he roomed with a business friend at a convention. He began to affirm at once that God was in control of everything about the situation and that the peace of Jesus Christ was all through his mind and emotions—and all through his friend's mind, body, and emotions too. Aloud he said the following affirmations:

"*The peace of Jesus Christ is all through you now. Your only reactions are peaceful. Your body and mind are at peace. There is perfect harmony and coordination in all your body functions. Divine order is at work now in your body and mind. You are all right. You are perfectly all right now. You are healed.*"

He put his hand on the man's shaking, convulsive body. He felt love going out from his body through his hands. His own fright was gone. He was calm in every way, and his friend was soon calm. A permanent healing began because his friend accepted suggestions for using affirmative prayer and anticipating the possibility of a complete healing.

"Great peace have they who love the Lord" came instantly to a mother's mind when one of her children went into convulsions. "And I do love the Lord," she thought, as she did the physical things she had been told to do to help alleviate the condition.

"You have great peace now," she said to the child time and time again. *"You love the Lord. He is healing you now. He is bringing about your perfect and complete healing now."*

In a few minutes the child was normal in all his body actions. His mother held him, glad that she was not feeling relief or exhaustion, only peace. The child soon slid off her lap and went back to his play. It was the last convulsion he ever had.

Skin

Our skin is our tent, the covering that describes the boundaries of our personal world. It separates us from everything outside of us. It is our protector, yet we are likely to take it for granted. Often we are hard on it. We expose it to all kinds of weather conditions and we ignore its needs. Most of us don't realize the many things it does for us.

The skin is a barometer of inner health conditions: when our digestive system is out of order a rash may appear to warn us and tell us what is going on inside. Welts can appear, telling us our emotions are out of tune. When nerves are uneasy our skin may itch and burn. For some of us our skin is an extrasensory "antenna." It acts as a warning signal if we are in danger: our skin may "crawl" before we are consciously aware of something menacing near us.

During our growing-up years we may have acne, thick skin, thin skin, rough skin, blotchy skin, spotted skin, sores. The skin is our buffer against the world. This means we must take both spiritual and physical care of this wonderful protecting "tent."

A woman healed herself of psoriasis, which had been a problem for many years, by blessing her skin and knowing that it did not matter that she had endured the burning and the itching for thirty years. It could clear, and it did. She used these words: *"My skin is perfectly smooth and free from any sores. God is healing it now."*

Another woman had never outgrown a severe acne condition. She started making herself "see" a clear complexion when she looked in her mirror. She had tried so many remedies, but none had worked. Now she decided to try God. *"God,"* she prayed, *"You're in charge of me and that includes my skin. I've done a terrible job of taking care of it. Thank You for making my skin beautiful now."*

Many things happened. Her work changed; her new job was close enough to her home that she could walk. She found that her taste was changing; she no longer craved foods that had seemed to be hard on her skin. A new neighbor moved in next door. She was a gardener. The first thing our lady-with-a-skin-problem knew, she too had a small vegetable and flower garden. The next thing she knew, her skin was free from new spots and old places were healing. She puts God in charge of all her healing needs now!

Love soothes rough skin that oils and lotions cannot heal. Pigmentation irregularities adjust when divine order is claimed. Rashes disappear when the peace of Jesus Christ is asked for.

Thank You, Father for my perfect skin. It is clear, smooth, perfect in every way. It is beautiful and wonderful. I am grateful for its protective care of my body. I bless it and take good care of it.

Strength

We need many different kinds of strengths. We always need all the physical strength we can accumulate, as well as mental strength, emotional strength, moral strength. Our greatest need is for spiritual strength, for through it comes all other strength. Sometimes we forget that our strength is always in the Lord. We forget how many times we are told in the Bible that the Lord will give us strength, that He *is* strength. We are told that He will renew our strength.

A little boy was lost in the woods. As the day passed he became very tired, so tired that he couldn't walk any farther. He was getting cold, he was afraid, and he was hungry. He didn't know which way he was going because the sky was overcast. Then he remembered to pray.

He prayed a very simple prayer: "*God, show me the way to go home. Give me strength to get there.*"

He sat down for a minute and thought about God and about his prayer. He looked up, and for a brief moment the sun almost came through the clouds. Only a minute—but long enough for the boy to know that he had been going in the wrong direction. He was so happy and so thankful that his tiredness dropped from him. He had hardly been able to walk before—now he could run!

A grandmother had five children to care for. She was running and doing, all day and often into the night. She was exhausted, but she still had a month to take care of them while a new business venture and new home were being established for the family. She knew she had to keep on, and she had to stop being so tired. Then she remembered that her strength came from her God. She had to pray "on the run," but she did so during the days and the nights: "*Father, thank You for all the strength I need right this moment.*"

She felt an inflow of new strength many times a day. The children became more helpful. There was more fun in being together. It became the happiest month of their lives.

A young mother had been ill. She needed strength so she could be up and doing for her children. All one night she prayed for strength and looked up Bible verses about strength. She felt better when she realized how many there were. It indicated to her that many people had had need for strength. She thought about strength, and about God as strength. An all-powerful God had to have strength, a loving God had to want to give her strength. She finally fell asleep feeling God's strength flowing into every part of her body. Sleepily, she said, "*Thank You, Father.*" When she awakened, she was able to get up and supervise the household and her children. She found that if she only turned within to the God of strength, she again felt this inflow of fresh, renewing vigor.

God's strength is available whenever we feel depleted or lacking in energy or strength. Whatever we have to do, we can have the strength to do it. God is strength, and He gives us all the strength we can possibly need. We do not have to feel tired, weak, lacking in energy; we can have this steady, dependable inflow of wonderful energy.

Surgery

Spiritual healing can hasten healing after surgery. It can help prevent complications. It can give the body newness and wholeness. Often spiritual healing can come in time to prevent surgery. Healing comes in many ways. Corrective surgery can help the body do its work more effectively and easily. Emergency surgery can take care of immediate situations that we have not been aware needed our healing attention. Always, no matter what we are doing to help the body, we need the perfect, complete healing only spiritual healing can bring. It makes all things easier, better.

Spiritual healing takes fear out of meeting a hospital experience. It makes us sure that God is in charge every minute: directing the minds and hands of surgeons, nurses, anesthetists, laboratory technicians, everyone concerned. It helps us know that everything that is being done or thought about us is as it should be and that perfect healing has already started in our body. It gets our mind, our emotion, and our body ready for perfect healing.

A man spent the afternoon before he went into the hospital knowing these things:

"There is only one Mind, not many minds, not the mind of the surgeon, the helpers, not even my mind, or the mind of my wife. Only one Mind, and that one Mind is taking care of this physical condition of my body perfectly and rapidly. Only right things are done. The healing is rapid and perfect; there are no complications. Some special blessing will come to everyone concerned in this situation, including me."

Surgery was successful, recovery rapid. His surgeon told him that he wished all of his patients healed as wonderfully and quickly as this man had.

Emergency surgery was done on a little girl. It was extremely difficult for her parents to keep their thoughts on the healing and not on the possible danger while the operation was in progress. They tried faithfully, and that is all we ever have to do. It became easier for them as time passed to affirm and to mean the prayer they had agreed to use:

"God is in charge of our daughter. We do not fear at all. God is in her body, God is in the mind and

hands of the doctor, the nurses, everyone who is helping her. God's healing love is already adjusting her body, cleansing, purifying, renewing, revitalizing, re-energizing, healing. Thank You, Father, for her perfect healing now."

As they prayed with feeling and meaning, their fear started to leave; they became calm and sure of the successful outcome. They rejoiced when they were told that all was well with their child. The little girl responded wonderfully to post-surgery treatment and went home much sooner than had been anticipated.

No, we do not leave God out of the operating room. He is there as He is everywhere. Whether we are there ourself or waiting with loving concern while a loved one is in that room, we can know that all is well, for God is in absolute control of all that is done. Healing is taking place. Healing can take place anywhere as we claim it.

Teeth

We need perfect teeth for more than chewing our food. Teeth make a difference to our general health, to our appearance. Every time we brush our teeth, we should say, "Thank You, Father, for these wonderful teeth that get food ready for my body's use, that help my face, that help me speak clearly." Teeth respond to love and appreciation; they respond to our healing thoughts.

A man was having difficulty with his gums. They seemed to be softening and loosening around his teeth. He was frightened about the possibility of having to have his teeth removed. He had had many small spiritual healings, and he believed that nothing was impossible to achieve with God's help. He began to praise his teeth for all they did and had done for him, and for all they would continue to do for his health and appearance.

Words of a familiar hymn came to him: "How firm a foundation." So he prayed happily: "*Father, thank You for a firm foundation for my teeth. My faith has a firm foundation, my belief in Your healing power has a firm foundation, my teeth have a firm foundation. My gums and my teeth are sound, whole, perfect now.*"

Soon his gums became sound and firm.

A young woman discovered that she had a large number of cavities. The dentist told her she must watch her diet. As she drove home she was thinking about changes in her diet, and she decided that she needed to watch her mental and emotional diet too. She had had one healing from using Truth; she didn't think that her teeth were any different from the rest of her body, so they would respond to Truth too.

She remembered what Paul said to the people in Iconium in recounting all that God had done for them, "(Satisfying) your hearts with food and gladness." The word *gladness* took her back to the account of the Pentecost, when Paul wrote that the people, "partook of food with glad and generous hearts." Singleness of heart she knew she would have if she gave God all the power in her life.

Gladness became her "theme song." She thought about gladness, she practiced feeling glad. She never ate anything that she didn't bless with a joy and understanding that her food, every bit of it, was healing, restoring, rebuilding her body. This included rebuilding her teeth. She tried to eat foods that had the food elements teeth need to build with; a hunger she had seemed to have all her life for sweets stopped. She was satisfied with other food, foods that were tooth-builders. She was happier than she had ever been before. Gladness became a way of life, a way of thinking, a way of feeling for her. At her next checkup there were no more cavities.

We are strong in the Lord; our teeth are strong in the Lord. We want only perfect food for our body; we chew it well; we eat it with joy and gladness. Our body responds with health, wholeness, soundness.

Vision

Our eyes show us things most of the twenty-four hours of each day. From the minute we are consciously awake until we go to sleep our eyes show us things that we need to see, understand, enjoy. When we lie down to sleep, the vision mechanism is not turned off. It takes us on journeys through our dreams. This inner seeing lets us see things past; it helps us picture the future. Often either the inner or outer vision, or both, need healing.

Sometimes our dreams are frightening, forbidding or foreboding. Sometimes what we see of the past or the future is not "healthy." Often we need to heal our perspectives. We don't always see things in their true light. We can be nearsighted when we see things only from our point of view, or neglect the long view; we can be so farsighted looking to the future that we overlook what is at hand.

We may have blurred vision, we may have astigmatism, our eyes may tend to cross, we may have an eye disease, we may have limited vision. Of all parts of the body, the eyes should respond most rapidly and wonderfully to Truth for the healing power has to be "seen," comprehended, understood—and it is through our eyes that we see and understand anything. Understanding is so close to seeing that when we get an idea, we say that we "see" it. The words "I see" are wonder-working words. They make a strong affirmative prayer for perfecting vision.

"I see. I see. I see perfectly. I see clearly. I see everything at hand, I see everything at a distance. I see with the eyes of Spirit. God sees the world through my eyes. I see the world through God's eyes in me. My eyes are healthy, they are whole. There is no limitation to my vision. I see everything God wants me to see. I see. I see. I see!"

When we start trying to see good in all things, all people, all happenings and circumstances, it can be amazing how much our eyesight improves. When we stop seeing all that is wrong with our fellow man and the world and start seeing what is right and good, we start to use God vision.

A woman had worn strong glasses for nearsightedness for many years. She had experienced several healings by using Truth ideas. She believed that there should be no difficulty in healing her eyes through spiritual methods. She wanted to be free from having to wear glasses all the time. She also knew that the outer, the physical, mirrors the inner; if she was going to be able to see farther and more clearly, she would have to expand her consciousness, see more good and good in more ways, always see the real and not the unreal, see God in all things, persons, and circumstances. These statements helped her:

"I reach to God. My vision reaches to God. God reaches out through my eyes to all people, to the world. Everything is clear to me as I see with the eyes of God. I am not fooled by anything; I know what is real and what is unreal. I see God everywhere. My true vision is spiritual, not physical. I do not see with my physical eyes. I see with my spiritual eyes and my vision is perfect now. Thank God!"

She refused to check on her progress; she held steadfastly to the conviction that her eyes were already perfect in Spirit and in Truth. One morning as she was preparing breakfast, one of the children asked, "Mother where are your glasses?" Her deepest desire had come true. She had awakened and had not had to reach out for her glasses. When she had her eyes checked some time later, her oculist was amazed and double-checked his findings to be sure he had made no mistake!

A man whose eyes crossed unless he wore corrective lenses had marked improvement (and finally healing) after he had declared and continued to declare that God could make the crooked straight and that he could let his "eyes look directly forward" and his "gaze be straight before" him. His condition improved to such an extent that he had to have his glasses refitted; the old ones bothered him. Within two years his miracle took place. The crooked had truly been made straight.

An eye infection left quickly when a young man came to know that God's healing power cleanses, purifies, removes anything unlike Him, and that God's healing is fast, sure, dependable, lasting.

We see with the eyes of Spirit. We see good everywhere, in everything and every person. We see God in, around, and part of all people and all things. Our inner vision is perfect, our outer vision is perfect too. Thank God!

Weight

The matter of weight and its distribution can be a recurring problem. Overweight, underweight, weight in the wrong places can make us unhappy and keep us from perfect health. Eating too much or too little, eating the wrong foods, impulsive eating, compulsive eating, eating to satisfy emotions, complicate the weight problem.

A man had been told that he must reduce to relieve the strain on his heart. He had tried before, many times, to reduce, but with little success. He was able to succeed after he used some Bible passages as his guide. He interpreted them for his own condition. His first inspiration came from Jesus' words: "Come to me, all who labor and are heavy laden, and I will give you rest." This man knew that he was making his body labor because he had let it get so heavy. *"God takes my heaviness from me and gives my body rest"* was his first prayer statement.

As he was reading his Bible another evening he found this in Ezekiel: "I will seek the lost [he had surely lost his figure], and I will bring back the strayed [certainly he had driven health and body perfection away with his overeating], and I will bind up the crippled [his determination not to eat], and I will strengthen the weak [his resolution to reduce needed a lot of strengthening], and the fat and the strong . . . I will feed them in justice [that was one thing he needed a lot of if he was going to get the reducing job done]."

He worked on good judgment and love: love for God and love for the body he had been given; judgment in choosing food and choosing quantities of food, and in exercise to tone the body. He started losing weight gradually and continuously.

A woman who knew that her desire for sweets caused a steady weight increase was able finally to control and direct her appetite when she constantly kept in mind that she desired only spiritual food and that Spirit satisfied her. Her almost insatiable appetite for sweets changed, and she started losing pounds in the right places.

For several years a woman had tried everything to gain weight. She tried many foods, many diets. The one that finally worked was a spiritual diet: *she took time to pray before she ate anything.* This uplifted her thought, relaxed her body, getting it ready for the food she ate and the liquids she drank. She blessed every bite.

She chewed more slowly, because it took time to bless each mouthful. She began to add pounds, she had renewed strength and energy, and new beauty. Her face lost its drawn look, her body formed some attractive curves, her skin looked healthier. Her whole body vibrated with health and happiness.

I have the perfect weight for my body. I do not overeat or undereat. I keep my emotions stable. I have no false desires for food. I want only that food and drink which is good for my body. I am satisfied with Spirit. My body is healthy and beautiful now. Thank God!

The Way It Can Be

It is exciting to know that we can generate health and create new body conditions. It is exciting to know that in us is this amazingly wonderful God-power, a true dynamo that we can start merely by thinking and feeling in the right way. When we do so, we feel a tingling as cells start working harmoniously and quickly to cleanse, purify, renew, restore body functions.

I am renewed and regenerated by the God-power within me. All power is given me, including power to heal. I have conscious control of my body and my health. I can turn on health.

We urge our body on to greater healthful activity by telling it that it is wonderful, for it is. Our words of healing turn on the generator: our blood circulates more freely, we breathe more deeply and more easily, tensions leave, we feel a new, buoyant lightness coupled with fresh strength. We know that the healing is not delayed, but is taking place now. We understand Isaiah better (38:8) for our healing "Shall spring up speedily." We feel the healing. We appreciate our body more and more.

We are wonderfully made, and we have been given power over the body through our thoughts, feelings, and words. Even though we have been thinking sick thoughts and have created sick body conditions, our wonderful body will respond to the right thoughts.

I am now free from wrong thoughts, feelings. I speak only health-bringing words. I think only health-filled thoughts. I expect health. Health and healing come.

This is the way we build a health consciousness and get rid of a sick consciousness. We picture the healing, expect the healing, know it is coming. We weed out old wrong thinking of the past. We eliminate all thoughts of injustice, self-pity, resentment, hate, hurt.

I am now free from anxiety, dread, remorse, hate. The cleansing, purifying, healing love of God now washes and dissolves any accumulation of error thoughts and error conditions. I am made new in mind and body.

We are not alarmed about any condition for we know that alarm aggravates any body need. We do not discuss it with other people for we know this makes healing more difficult, because it puts us in contact with the negative thoughts of others.

It is our thought of the appearance that must be healed first. We keep our mind stayed on God and His omnipotence. We keep our mind on the healing.

I am not disturbed by an appearance of sickness because I have faith in God's healing power. I can use this power no matter where I am or what is wrong. I trust Him to make me whole, perfect, strong now.

We are not alarmed even if there is an unnatural growth, for we know that our only true growth is spiritual. Instead of being upset, we find our peace. Healing takes place as we know this peace of God. Often it comes as a kind of crystal moment, a bright moment in our conscious thought. In this crystal moment, there is no thought of the physical condition. There is no thought of the healing. There is only peace. Sometimes we feel God's loving, healing power. Sometimes we feel that we are channels, and we visualize ourself as a channel. Some of us feel God's hand soothing, healing, supporting.

God's peace is mine. God's peace is healing my body now.

New cells continuously form. Our conscious minds accept this fact and our subconscious mind creates the new cells. We know that God's healing power can "turn on the lights" in our cells, can "start the music playing." With our thoughts, our feelings, and our words we transform our body. We send our healing word to the depths of our being and every cell responds. We decree health to our body in the name and through the power of Jesus Christ, who knew so completely that He and the Father were one that the Father could do His perfect healing work through Him. Jesus Christ promised us that we could do the same, and we can. He said that we would be able to do even more than He did. His ministry was only three years long; ours can be much, much longer.

Through the power of Jesus Christ my cells are all new and whole. My body sings with health. My body is filled with light, wonderful healing light.

We need to find the healing word that is *our* word. We may find our own special word among the following that have helped bring healings for many people:

God in the midst of me is mighty to heal me perfectly right now.

My body is spiritual substance. I let it express its perfection now. Infinite perfection is now working in my body, unhindered by me. I consciously direct it to do its healing work now without delay.

My health is God's business. No one, no thing, no condition can interfere with the healing.

I give thanks for my perfect health (healing) now.

I am free from mistakes and consequences of mistakes in thinking, feeling, speaking, and action. All effects of these errors are erased, dissolved, healed.

I get ready for health (healing). I place my life in God's hands. I plan all that I do and say in Truth.

When I hear of a healing, I rejoice, for I know that what God does for others, He will do for me.

I work Truth into every part of my body, for I know that my body is the result of all my thinking and feeling and I want it perfect in the future.

I never doubt that any condition can be healed with God's help.

I work always for the whole man. The whole man is God's man—perfect, healthy, wonderful.

Even when we are not sick or in need of a physical healing, we feel God's life in us continuously restoring our bodies, making them perfect. We feel our perfect spiritual freedom.

I am free to choose health, to choose divine order, to praise and bless my body. I am free to be healthy.

I am young, healthy, strong. My body outpictures my perfect health now.

We stand firm in our belief in our healing. We stand firm knowing all the time that it is never we who do the healing work. We stand firm because we are ever in the Presence. We do not treat our body; we treat our thoughts and feelings. We treat to bring forth our real Self, our spiritual Self. The Self is there, perfect and whole, always waiting for us to call it out.

As we work we are sensitive only to good; we are not affected by any outer appearances. We never let our inner peace leave us. We know that the sickness or condition needing healing is not true, no matter how actual it may appear. We know that nothing is too bad for God's healing power to take care of and make right.

All conditions are open to the possibility of God's healing.

Health is my divine right. I expect it and I accept it now!

Study Guide

Understanding comes with study. Faithfulness to study pays unlimited dividends. These questions based on each of the chapters of the first part of *Healing Now* are planned to help the student get the most from his study of the book. It is suggested that the reader go over the questions before reading a chapter. This helps him know what he is going to learn.

After studying a chapter, many students find it helpful for later study to write the answers in the book after each question; others write them in a notebook or on cards.

The last part of the book can be studied in a similar way. Before the reader studies the section he is interested in, he can formulate his own questions to help him be sure that he gets all possible help from his reading.

I. Healing Is Possible: Health Is a Divine Right

1. What is the Truth that heals?
2. What is our spiritual self? Does it help healing?
3. What molds and repairs our physical body?
4. How is healing done?
5. Why is this hard for us to understand?
6. What is God's will in our sickness?
7. How do we cooperate?
8. Do I believe God sends suffering?
9. What does God's good for us include?
10. Why did Moses give so many health laws?
11. How does sin affect health? Emotions? Thinking?
12. Memorize three Biblical promises of healing. Why is this good to do?
13. How do we know that our body is made for healing?
14. What did Marge do to bring about her healing?
15. What can be healed in our life?

Yes, we have the divine possibility for healing NOW.

II. Wanting to Be Sick

1. Why would I ever want to be sick?
2. Do I have a sick consciousness?
3. What starts a sick consciousness? What feeds it?
4. Do I ever postpone a healing? Why?
5. Do I need pampering?
6. Do I want to get away from work, responsibility?
7. What can we learn from Ethel Barrymore?
8. Why do we need emotion-charged denials and affirmations to start the healing process?
9. Do I have many big or little accidents? As I think about an accident I had, I ask myself: Was I emotionally involved at the time? Was I tired? Did I want it to happen? Why?
10. What do our words have to do with our accidents, our health?
11. If I need a healing now, do I really want it? Will a healing now make me have to start doing things I don't really want to do?
12. Am I kidding myself about my health, in any way?
13. Do I believe I have the power of choice: health or sickness?
14. What do I really want?

Today I choose health.

III. Prevention and Cure

1. What do we need to think about before we think about prevention?
2. What causes illness? Accidents?
3. What are we likely to be forgetting?
4. What is the work of our subconscious? What is its main desire? What are its limitations?
5. What is the power of the conscious mind?
6. How can the conscious and subconscious minds work together to prevent and heal dis-ease?
7. Where does our preventive work begin?
8. How can I improve my body? Is my body static?
9. Do I think that God has all power in my body or do I believe that sickness, another power, is taking over my body?
10. How do we turn on the healing power in us?
11. What does it mean to look to the healing first?
12. How is the healing done?
13. How do prevention and cure work together? What makes them a team?
14. Who is the healer?

My conscious mind decides what is given to my subconscious. I give my subconscious thoughts of strength, healing, happiness, joy, good. I consciously erase all negative thoughts, all disease breeding thoughts and emotions. I am now in control of what goes into my subconscious.

IV. Delayed or Incomplete Healing: Instantaneous or Complete

1. What is part of the answer to getting complete and instantaneous healing?
2. What small word should we eliminate from our vocabulary? Why?
3. How can our thought about time delay our healing?
4. If healing doesn't come quickly or completely, what do we do?
5. What do we do about fear?
6. Name three ways we can overcome delays in healing.
7. How can listening to guidance after prayer help bring about healing?
8. How can we get out of the way of our healing? How do we often interfere with our healing?
9. How can we "abandon ourself to God?" What happens when we do?
10. How do we "let" our healing happen?

I cease to be concerned about my healing, whether it takes a long time or a short time. I release my healing to God and let it happen.

V. The Holy Temple: Its Care

1. How do we use our body? Do we ever abuse it?
2. What has religion done to our thought about our body?
3. Why must we keep our mind, body, and emotions perfect?
4. What difference will it make in us when we fully realize that our body is truly the temple of the living God?
5. How will we know what to do to keep it perfect?
6. When will a super race appear?
7. What is one way to show our love for God?
8. What makes the music in our temple?
9. What lights the temple?
10. Why should we appreciate our body?
11. What is the most important fact about our body?
12. Do we listen to ourselves in our temple? If not, to whom?

I know that my body is the temple of the living God. I take care of it, I protect it, I bless it.

VI. Healing Habits

1. Do we have any habits we want to heal?
2. When does a habit need healing?
3. Do I have any habits that control my life, decide what I do?
4. Is it possible that I kid myself about my habits? Am I afraid or ashamed to admit that I am slave to a habit?
5. Why was it easier for Jack to ask his angel to help?
6. Can we imagine ourself getting to the place where we too can enjoy the game of breaking a bad habit as Jack did?
7. Do we have to break our habit alone? Do we ever have to do anything alone?
8. Are we refusing to listen when others try to point out to us what a habit or habits are doing to us?
9. How could it help Nell to think of her habit as a sickness? Could it be easier for us to think of a habit we don't want as an illness, rather than a habit?
10. Do we honestly expect a healing for our habit?
11. Do we think that we have to continue to be enslaved?
12. How do we start and where do we go to get help in healing a habit we don't want? Is it difficult to get help?
13. What were the four things the ten-year-old did to bring about his healing? Can we use the same four?

I know the habit that needs healing. God is helping me heal it right now. I expect the healing and it comes. Thank God!

VII. Healing Relationships

1. What is meant by a "who" and a "what" making us sick?
2. Do we have any people in our life who are making us sick now?
3. When should we suspect that some relationship is making us sick?
4. What did Dorothy's doctor mean when he asked if something were "eating at her"?
5. Do we ever think to "gather up our peace" before we meet people we find difficult?
6. Can we too use "peace magic"? What is it?
7. Where do we use "spiritual magic" first?
8. What does this magic change in us?
9. Who must be in charge of our relationships?
10. Can we get to the place where we become aware of sick relationships early, before they do any damage to us and our body?
11. How do we protect ourself if we are "dropped" into a sick situation?
12. Do we ever pray that other people change?
13. Does time have anything to do with healing?
14. Do we ever have moments when we too feel that we are not on good terms with the Father? If we feel this, what do we do?

I am at peace with all people. All people are at peace with me. I am on good terms with God every minute. I am on good terms with the world. I express nothing but peace; I experience nothing but peace.

VIII. Healing Memories

1. What do we have to search out first when we have a need for healing?
2. What memories bless? Which ones burn?
3. What do we do about memories of unhappiness, resentment, injustice?
4. What did one man do to keep himself free from emotional reactions to unpleasantness?
5. How do we start to find our memories that need healing?
6. How does our subconscious operate with our memories?
7. Why does it change our desires and reactions? Why doesn't it let us see ourself as we really are?
8. What can we expect when we start to heal our memories?
9. How must we react to the unhappy memories we begin to remember? Should we be ashamed? Afraid?
10. How can we rid ourself of the hurtful influence of any memory?
11. Does a memory have to be uncovered and recalled before it can be healed?
12. What three things happen when we heal a memory?
13. Can all memories be healed?
14. What do we do about memories we are storing in our subconscious now?

I release and let go all old, hurting memories. I learn from them if I can. I bless them. They no longer affect my life. I am free from their influence. Thank God, I am free for new good now.

IX. Healing Failure

1. What is the wonderful truth about us in relation to failure?
2. How does it help when we start thinking about our failures as sicknesses?
3. Is it good to look at our failures objectively?
4. Can we learn anything about our own failures from Morgan's story?
5. How did Henry heal his "permanent" failure?
6. Can it be a good thing to be tired of failing?
7. What was the jolting idea for George? What did he learn about his responsibility for his failure and for his success?
8. How can it help us if we don't feel that we alone are responsible for our success or failure?
9. Is it easy to think that everything is against us? What can we do to heal this feeling? What did Dale do?
10. What was the first thing Dale did to start changes in his life? Can we do similar things in our life now?
11. What was his basic decision?

I can be through with failure. God takes over for me. I do what He wants me to do and I rapidly become a success. I get in tune with success. Success is attracted to me because I am through with failure forever. I look successful, I act successful. I am successful now. Thank God!

X. Healing Finances

1. Where and how do we start healing our finances?
2. Can we actually be (right now) richer than we think? What does credit really mean?
3. What sick financial attitudes did Jim heal?
4. To what should we give our attention? Our money? Our lack of money? Our income? Our debts?
5. What does changing our mind have to do with healing our finances? Where does any healing have to start?
6. What did Art learn from Joseph? Can we learn too?
7. Did the Patriarchs have problems? How did they solve them?
8. What about tithing?
9. Is the tithe a "financial thank you" to God? Is the tithe to pay bills?
10. What has fear to do with lack? Can fear cut off our flow of money? Are we keeping a perfect inflow and outflow of money? Why should we?
11. Where does our money come from, anyway?
12. How do we heal our finances and keep them well?

God is my instant, constant, unlimited Supply. He is the Source of my income. I remember the Lord for it is He who has power to make me rich. I am the child of a rich Father who provides abundantly for me now and always.

XI. Healing Others

1. What is the first healing rule Ann learned? The second?
2. What did Ann have to relearn about looking at physical appearances?
3. What has to happen to us before we can heal?
4. What did the little family learn about how to heal?
5. How long do we have to wait before we can help others with their healing needs?
6. Why is it good that we never have to do the healing?
7. What do we have to know?
8. To Whom do we go for the healing?
9. Is there a healing law of life and wholeness? How do we get the law to work?
10. What happens when we turn from appearances?
11. What is our part in the healing?
12. Why is it necessary for us to be calm, very still inside and out?
13. Where do we keep our attention all the time?

I turn from the horror and hurt to the healing. I pay no attention at all to appearances. I expect a healing without delay, and it comes. Thank God!

XII. Healing Can Be Permanent

1. What is our special good news?
2. What do we have to be sure about?
3. What do we do?
4. What does standing firm have to do with healing?
5. What does expectancy have to do with healing?
6. What harm can be done by thinking healing won't last?
7. Where does permanent healing have to be first?
8. How can we share our healing knowledge with many people?
9. Can we actually serve mankind with this knowledge?
10. What does it mean to turn from the horror to the healing?
11. Are we the healers? Or are we the knowers? What is a knower?
12. How can we "rise above" health needs?
13. Where do we keep our mind? Our attention?
14. What is the only thing we have to be concerned with?
15. What do we have to know?
16. What should be our healing goal?

My permanent healing comes now in God's wonderful way.

PRINTED U.S.A.

109F-10M-1-71